W9-ADM-254

The Essentials of Business Writing

A Simple Guide for Writing It Right —
Every Time!

Edited by National Press Publications

NATIONAL PRESS PUBLICATIONS

A Division of Rockhurst University Continuing Education Center, Inc.
6901 West 63rd Street • P.O. Box 2949 • Shawnee Mission, Kansas 66201-1349
1-800-258-7248 • 1-913-432-7757

The Essentials of Business Writing

Published by National Press Publications, Inc.
Copyright 2000 National Press Publications, Inc.
A Division of Rockhurst University Continuing Education Center, Inc.

Printed in the United States of America

 2 3 4 5 6 7 8 9 10

ISBN 1-55852-267-0

Table of Contents

FOREWORD

The world of writing has come a long way from the quill-and-parchment, fountain pen-and-vellum, even ballpoint-and-paper methods used to communicate from person to person. Today, computers are used for most of your business correspondence. Data, text and graphics networks make it possible for you to communicate complex ideas with people all over the world. Sophisticated software solves your spelling conundrums, and grammar software seeks out your most glaring errors.

Despite all these technological advances, the idea for any writing must still originate in the brain of a human being — you. You are the one who determines the content, organization, wording and format of the information you wish to send. You are the one who is ultimately responsible for the message that you send.

Often, that message will ultimately decide what kind of impression you leave with your reader. If you send a poorly worded, badly edited message, your reader may decide that you are someone who is careless, sloppy, or worse, illiterate. A well-thought-out, correct message can make the difference in getting the job interview, making the sale or putting yourself on the promotion ladder. You simply can't afford to settle for anything less than perfect, every time.

This handbook is designed to make it easy for you to do just that. From the first moment when you conceive the idea, begin to organize your thoughts and put the words into some sort of structure, to the final editing, proofreading and correction stages, you'll easily be able to pick up the information where and when you need it in your correspondence process.

1 OVERVIEW OF THE WRITING PROCESS

"English usage is sometimes more than mere taste, judgment, and education. Sometimes it's sheer luck, like getting across the street."

— E.B. White

Don't Make It Difficult: Four Simple Rules to Simplify the Writing Task

Rule 1: No First Draft Masterpieces

A sculptor makes a few sketches of what he's going to create, then makes a small clay model before doing the full-scale piece. An engineer has the plan of the bridge set down on paper and in his head before he puts up the lasting steel.

When you're working on a long or complex piece of writing, you should do the same. Get a plan in front of you and do some drafting before you produce your final version.

Rule 2: One Job at a Time

Keep separate jobs separate. Don't proofread, look up correct spellings or worry about punctuation while you're drafting a first version. Just capture your thoughts on paper. When you have your thoughts on paper, then you can polish, correct and shorten the work.

Don't try to revise your writing when you or someone else is doing the final keyboarding. That leads to endless numbers of "final" versions, and neither you nor your typist will do them with proper care because you both expect there will be another "final" version.

Drafting, revising, typing and proofreading are separate jobs that need their own kind of attention and their own time. Keep them separate.

Rule 3: Write for Minutes, Not Hours

How long can you concentrate on a piece of business reading? Whatever length of time that may be, cut it in half to find out how long you can keep your concentration on your writing. If you can read business materials for 30 minutes before your concentration slips, then you can probably write for about 15 minutes before you need a break.

Yes, you could write for two or three hours if you had to, but would your work be as good in the last half-hour as it was in the first? Most people write best if they take a break every 10-20 minutes. Others are most productive when they stay on a roll for five minutes, take a short break, then come back and write for another five minutes. Find your best pace and don't worry about looking busy every minute. When you are writing, activity doesn't always equal productivity. Some of your best ideas come from leaning back, staring at the ceiling and thinking.

Rule 4: Be a Good Boss to Yourself

Suppose your boss took you by the scruff of your neck, pointed to a chair, told you to sit down and write something by four o'clock, and said, "And it better be perfect, too." We tend to do that to ourselves when we face a writing job.

Imagine how others would react if you did that to them. They would feel resentment, low motivation and reluctance to work unless someone stood over them with a whip! And isn't that how you often feel when confronted with a writing job?

Give yourself:

- Reasonable deadlines with time to do a good job

- A clear idea of the purpose of the writing

- An understanding of how the job is to be done

- The right materials for efficient work

An Easy Writing Method You Can Use

Do you panic when you must write a report, memo or letter? Do you feel confused with how to put your thoughts into words, how to handle the mechanics of style, how to deal with grammar, spelling and syntax? If you're one of these people, relax. Here is an easy method that you can use for any kind of correspondence from fax to e-mail, from memo to letter.

The method has three basic steps of writing:

1. Prewriting

2. Freewriting

3. Rewriting (or editing)

1. Prewriting

The first step involves preparing yourself to write. How long you spend at this stage is determined by:

- How well you know the subject

- How well you know the reader

In this first stage, you will spend time determining exactly what you hope to accomplish with your correspondence, why you are writing, who will read your correspondence, and what actions or events you expect to occur. This is the time to do any research, gather any facts or review past correspondence.

In this stage, you create an outline of what you want to say, using either the standard outline methods or other organizational methods such as clustering. Once you have an outline — anything from two or three lines to two or three pages — you can move to the second stage.

2. Freewriting

At this stage, you will put your ideas onto the paper in sentence form. Many writers make the common mistake of believing that this first draft must also be correct. They try to get it right the first time. In fact, it takes longer to try to write a perfect first draft than it does simply to get the ideas onto the paper and then go on to rewrite and edit the draft.

The most important part of this stage is actually getting the ideas into a form that you can work with. You'll write it quickly, without too much thought for elegant expressions, final order or paragraph divisions.

Many people prefer to do this stage of writing with pen and paper, but if you are proficient with your keyboard, then you can also do it on the computer. Whatever method you use, just let the words flow — start in the middle or the end, do the introduction later, fill in the gaps in information when you rewrite. Keep writing until you have completed the first draft.

3. Rewriting (or Editing)

In this stage, you'll read the draft several times, checking for style, grammar, spelling and syntax. Using a systematic process, you'll be able to ensure that your final product is correct in every way.

You'll want to make sure that your work reads easily, that it is clear and easy to understand, and that it conveys the information you want it to.

Then, as you look over your correspondence in its final form, you'll take a few minutes to proofread for all those little errors that no spelling or grammar program will catch.

Summary — Three Simple Steps and Ten Stages to Error-Free Writing

Here's a brief checklist of the three basic steps to writing it right, every time.

Step One: Prewriting

1. Identify and state your purpose.

2. Know your audience.

3. Define the scope of your subject.

4. Conduct research and gather data.

5. Organize the data and devise a rough plan.

6. Outline your writing project.

Step Two: Freewriting

7. Write the first draft.

Step Three: Rewriting

8. Edit and rewrite the draft for clarity, tone, accuracy and brevity.

9. Check for grammar and spelling errors and other careless mistakes.

10. Make sure the final copy is neat, error-free and ready to go.

How comfortable are you with the writing process? Take a few minutes to complete this self-analysis and find out your writing strengths and weaknesses. Put a check mark under the answer appropriate to your writing style.

	Never	Sometimes	Always
1. I have to get it right the first time. I don't have time for editing and rewriting.			
2. I keep my dictionary right beside my workspace and stop to look up the words as I write.			
3. I revise my writing over and over again. There's always one more revision to be done.			
4. I stick with my writing task until it's done, even if I'm tired or finding it hard to concentrate.			
5. I set tight deadlines for my writing. That forces me to get to it and stick to it — no matter what!			
6. I feel really panicked when I'm suddenly faced with a writing task.			
7. I generally just wade right into the writing and hope it will sort itself out as I write.			

Reflections

	Never	Sometimes	Always

8. I never bother with outlines and things, even for big jobs. They just take a lot of time and effort that I don't have.

9. I use the "spell checker" feature on my word processor only if I'm unsure about a spelling. Otherwise, I don't bother since I'm a pretty good speller.

10. I figure most people don't know where a comma should go either, so I don't worry too much about little bits of punctuation.

Scoring:
Always: 1 check mark
Sometimes: 3 check marks
Never: 5 check marks

10-20: You're making your writing task a lot harder than it needs to be. Using the ideas in this book will take the burden of writing off you and give you the freedom to become a good, fast, efficient writer.

21-35: You have some good writing habits, but there are several areas where you can improve your writing skills.

36-50: You're probably an efficient writer already. Using this handbook will give you the extra edge you need to become a top-notch business writer.

Reflections
Reflections

2 PREWRITING — GETTING READY TO WRITE

"I write when I'm inspired, and I see to it that I'm inspired at nine o'clock every morning."

— Peter De Vries

Unless you're aiming for the Nobel Prize, you shouldn't be concerned about your writing talent. Writing good business documents is a craft, not an art. It requires skill, not talent, and you can learn skills.

Before you begin to write anything, you need to set the stage for yourself.

Think of Yourself as a Communicator, Rather Than a Writer

Many business writers get hung up on the idea that they must become writers in order to communicate ideas.

Again, we're not talking Nobel Prizes here. We're simply talking about writing information in a way that makes it possible for other people to read that information and use it in the way you want them to. That's it.

Your job is to communicate: to organize a chaotic swarm of ideas and to communicate those ideas to others in an orderly and understandable fashion.

Set Aside Time to Write

How many times have you tried to write that important letter or memo in between phone calls, meetings or interruptions? It doesn't work, does it? Writing takes time — not a lot of time — but concentrated time. If you are going to communicate ideas to other people, you need to plan on giving yourself time to do just that.

How much time will you need? Using the three-step system of prewriting, freewriting and rewriting, you can do with as little time as ten minutes. But those must be ten uninterrupted minutes. If you have the luxury, 20 minutes is better, and half an hour is better still. You'll want to take a break after half an hour. That's about as much time as the average person can manage in the concentrated process of writing (although prolific fiction writers like Stephen King are known to write nonstop for hours at a time!).

When's the best time to write? That depends on you. If you're a morning person, find some time in the morning when you're least likely to be interrupted. Go in to work early if you can and set aside the time for writing. If you're an evening person, spending half an hour in the evening is more productive for you than wasting several fruitless hours in the afternoon, trying to write that pending memo. If you're a late-afternoon person, someone who turns into a zombie after lunch, set aside that last half-hour before quitting time. The impending deadline will add some urgency to your writing, and your energy level will be refreshed from your downtime in the afternoon.

Avoid Interruptions

Whatever you do, close your door and put your calls on hold. This is time that you have chosen to do one thing and one thing only — communicate in writing.

"I can't do that," you may say. "I don't have a door. I have to answer my calls. I have to be available to my staff." You might like to try the system used by some business writers. They take their lunch hour later and use the staff lunch hour to do their writing. Or do the same with the coffee break. While everyone else is down in the cafeteria, you're at your desk, getting the writing done. Then, you can reward yourself with a quiet cup of coffee later.

Be Disciplined

The best way to develop a sense of discipline is to do your writing at the same time every day. Instead of trying to answer your letters, e-mails and memos as you receive them, save them for your specific writing time. Then, answer them without fail.

To make this easier for yourself, read all your correspondence with a pen in hand. Jot down your ideas and comments in the margin, or underline the important points. Then, when it comes time to reply, you'll find the writing is faster and easier to do.

Are you ready to become a business writing professional? Test yourself to find out.

	Never	Sometimes	Always
1. Do you feel that business writing should be left to the "real" writers — people who get paid to write?			
2. Do you do your writing tasks whenever you have time or whenever they come up?			
3. Do you try to get your writing done and handle phone calls, meetings and other interruptions at the same time?			
4. Do you answer e-mails, faxes, memos, letters, etc. as they come across your desk?			
5. Do you see writing as a burdensome chore that has to be done?			

Where you have answered "always" in these questions, you're making writing more difficult for yourself. By moving away from these writing positions toward a new writing practice, you'll find that your writing will become better, and you will begin to enjoy the writing process.

Reflections

Take a few minutes now and reflect on the best time of the day for you to do your writing tasks.

- Are you a morning person — raring and ready to go at the crack of dawn? Consider coming in earlier to do your writing.

- Do you rev up in the middle of the morning? Skip or delay the midmorning coffee break and give yourself some good writing time.

- Are you ready to go at it in the afternoon? Take an early lunch and then settle into your writing tasks.

- Do you really get moving at the end of the day? Stay a little later and do your writing when everyone else has gone home.

- Are you a night owl? Perhaps you can work out a time-sharing deal with your boss so that you can work in the evening.

Try to schedule your writing at the most efficient time of the day for you.

Reflections

3 PREWRITING — KNOW YOUR AUDIENCE

"I'm always, always trying to interpret Life in terms of lives, never just in terms of characters."

— Eugene O'Neill

Who Is Your Reader?

No one will dispute that it's important for you to know what you're writing about, but in order to get that information across to another person, it's equally important to know who is going to read your writing. The better you know your reader, the more effective you will be in influencing him.

Writing is communication. When your writing fails to meet your readers' needs, you've failed to communicate. A clear sense of whom you are writing to is essential for successful communication. Organize and present your ideas with a targeted reader in mind.

For example, if you're writing about the company's year-end performance, you would write a different report to the vice president of sales, the marketing manager, the president of the company or the stockholders. Each reader would want to know different types of information and would have different levels of expertise. You need to tailor your message to the level and to the interests of your audience.

Ask yourself eight questions when considering your audience:

1. What should readers know or be able to do after reading your message?

2. What is their level of understanding or expertise regarding the subject?

3. Do you want to persuade them to do or accept something?

4. What are their interests and motivations — profit, comfort, health, convenience, savings, security?

Don't stop there. Ask:

5. What do my readers want to know?

6. What do my readers need to know?

7. What are their biases, their blind spots?

8. What decisions will be based on what I tell them?

Consider these points:

1. If you're trying to get agreement on a proposal or budget, you'll need to know your readers' current views on these matters.

2. If you're writing to increase their knowledge, you need to know how much they already know.

3. If you're trying to change how they do something, you may have to know why they use their present methods.

4. If you're trying to get action, you need to know what motivates them.

Knowing your readers so that you can convince them doesn't mean that you should deceive them, however. Above all, retain trust and integrity in your dealings with your readers.

Write With One Person in Mind

It's hard to write to someone you don't know. An easy technique to make your writing more readable and understandable is to write as if you were writing to someone you know.

- If you're writing a memo to six people, and you know one of those people, write as if you were writing to that person. If you're writing a memo to six people, and you know them all, write as if you were writing to the one who knows the least about the subject of your memo. In doing so, you will give full information to all your readers.

- If you're writing to a group of people (such as the general shareholders), think of someone you know who would fit into their category: age, gender, occupation, interests, etc. That person may not be a general shareholder, but by writing with him in mind, you immediately add a personal flavor to your correspondence that makes it more effective.

- If you're writing to a large segment of the population (such as government bulletins), write as if writing to your Aunt Sally, your mother or your sister. Write to one person. Otherwise, your writing is impersonal, cold and formal in style.

Put Yourself in Their Shoes

Finally, imagine yourself as the reader. Ask yourself these questions:

1. What do I want to know from this correspondence?

2. What kind of language is comfortable for me to read?

3. How much do I already know about this subject?

4. Why would I want to read this correspondence?

5. What do I want to do after reading this correspondence?

Before you begin to write, always take a few moments and think about the reader. Doing this at the beginning will save you endless frustration later, will make your style more readable, and will give your reader a real reason to read your correspondence. Neglecting this simple step results in a business communication that is impersonal and far less effective.

You've been asked to write a proposal for flextime working hours in your company. How would you slant the material to suit:

1. The board of directors?

2. Your boss?

3. Your co-workers?

4. The union?

Reflections
Reflections

4 PREWRITING — KNOW YOUR SUBJECT

"The greatest part of a writer's time is spent in reading, in order to write ... ."

— Dr. Samuel Johnson

The more you know about your subject, the better you'll be able to write about it. It's as simple and as complex as that!

Ask yourself, "What is the purpose of this message? Why am I writing it?" From this, ask yourself, "What do I want to say? What is the scope of my subject?" The answers to these questions determine the information you will need for your writing.

Researching

The amount of research required will vary greatly, depending on the subject and the purpose. In general, you have five basic sources of information:

1. **Libraries** — specialized, public and industry-specific libraries

2. **Other people** — interviews with experts, questionnaires, surveys, etc.

3. **Industry and government** — industry associations and groups, government agencies and officials

4. **Your own company** — files, history, personnel, etc.

5. **Your own knowledge** — experience, training, education

Your research may be as brief as jotting down sales figures from memory or as lengthy as several weeks or months of gathering data for a report on new site locations. Replying to customer inquiries or complaints can involve research lasting from a few minutes to several days or weeks.

When gathering information, remember the three cardinal rules of journalism: *accuracy, accuracy, accuracy*. Make sure you copy or quote information exactly and have the data to support your statements. Nothing loses a reader's confidence in a writer's work more quickly than discovering errors in the material.

Organizing

How you organize your material depends on your subject and your purpose for writing. For example, if you're giving instructions on machine assembly, you would choose a step-by-step approach to explain how to put the machine together. If you're making a special offer to a customer or breaking bad news to a client, you would put the most important information first and then fill in the details. Each type of letter or report has a specific purpose that will determine how you organize and arrange the material.

You've been asked to put together a report on the pros and cons of working with flextime in an organization. Your organization doesn't currently use flextime.

What are some sources of information you could use to find data for your report?

1.

2.

3.

4.

5.

6.

7.

8.

9.

10.

Reflections

5 PREWRITING — OUTLINING

*"When schemes are laid in advance, it is surprising
how often the circumstances fit in with them."*

— Sir William Osler

Your outline may consist of a few main points you wish to cover or a more detailed breakdown of each point.

Traditional Outline Form

The traditional way to outline is to break the subject down into its **P**arts, **P**hases, **P**roblems or **P**oints (the four P's) and assign priority to the items. There are four steps to this method:

1. List the P's in the order of their importance. (Here's where the formulas come in handy.)

2. Under each main P, arrange supporting ideas in the order of their importance.

3. Ensure that everything in your outline is relevant.

4. Check the order of your topics again.

Here's an example of how a traditional outline would look. The subject of this report to the management is "Upgrading to a New Computer System for the Office and Implementing It Within the Company."

I. Survey office staff.
  A. Poll attitudes toward computer systems currently in use.
      1. Questionnaire to be distributed by H.R. staff.
      2. Answers to be compiled by Tech Support Group.
  B. Determine levels of skills and experience.
      1. Standardized testing to be carried out by H.R. staff.
      2. Results compiled and analyzed by H.R. staff.
  C. Analyze workflow.
      1. Conduct one-week, on-site observations.
      2. Create standard form for measurement.
  D. Analyze individual job responsibilities —
     carried out by H.R. staff.
      1. Use current job descriptions.
      2. Revise as needed.
      3. Note any overlap.

II. Research best computer system.
  A. Consult with H.R. to determine software needs.
  B. Determine best hardware.
  C. Survey plant outlets, power lines, electrical capacity,
     lighting, etc.
      1. Work with Engineering staff.
          i) Note current usage.
          ii) Note any additional needs.
      2. Request estimates from Engineering.

III. Do cost analysis.
  A. Analyze comparative costs of hardware/software configurations.
  B. Determine cost of maintenance, supplies.
  C. Estimate costs of training staff.

IV. Establish installation and training schedule.

And so it goes on. You can see that this is a very comprehensive outline with all the information in place. The report should practically write itself!

However, doing an outline like this takes a lot of time. Wouldn't it be better if you could organize your thoughts and ideas in one quick, easy step, rather than trying to write the perfect outline before you even begin? Here is a more user-friendly technique that is a lot faster and easier to do.

The Clustering Method Outline

The inherent problem with the traditional outline method is that it deals with a vertical chain of thought — from 1, to 2, to 3, and so on. Our brains don't work that way. Our brains, especially when we're creating ideas, tend to jump all over the place. How often have you spent hours arranging and rearranging an outline, all because your ideas didn't automatically fall into a logical progression of thought?

Let's look at a way that allows your brain to access ideas at random and get them down on paper. Once you've got your ideas captured, then you can take a few minutes to arrange them in priority sequence.

Using the clustering method also allows you to spend a lot less time on the outlining phase of prewriting. You can do a quick cluster in five minutes and then walk away from it. Come back 20 minutes later and do another 5 minutes of clustering. Organize what you have. Come back later and add some more. Carry cluster-sheets with you and use them during downtime: waiting at the doctor's office, on hold on the telephone, between meetings.

Here's how it works:

1. **Write your topic or idea in the middle of a blank sheet of paper.** You won't be able to do this on your computer, but it's so fast and easy that using paper is much more convenient. Get in the habit of carrying a notebook with you. You can cluster while waiting for the bus, eating your lunch or anytime an idea comes to you.

2. **Draw a circle around the word you've written.** This gives the page some form and function and allows the left, logical side of your brain to relax while your right, creative brain lets the ideas flow.

3. **Sit back and relax.** This is the hardest part of clustering. Don't worry about what you're going to write. Just think about the word in the middle of the page.

4. **Record your thoughts.** As ideas come to you about that word in the middle of the page, jot them down anywhere on the page. Try to keep them to one or two words. Circle the words and join them with a line to whatever triggered the thought.

Here's an example of how clustering might work, using the same topic as the example for the traditional outline.

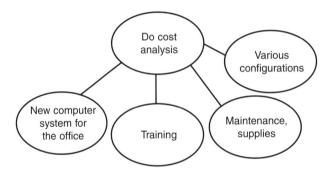

The first step was to jot down the main thought in the middle of the page, "new computer system for the office," which was then circled. Then, the author thought of the need to do a cost analysis. Note that the first idea to come to mind was not the first idea listed in the traditional outline. Using this method, you don't have to worry whether your first idea will be the most important one or not.

After getting this thought, the author decided that the cost analysis should be done on the various configurations, the training, and the maintenance and supplies. Note that there is very little detail in these thoughts — just the main idea is jotted down.

Now, let's take it a little further.

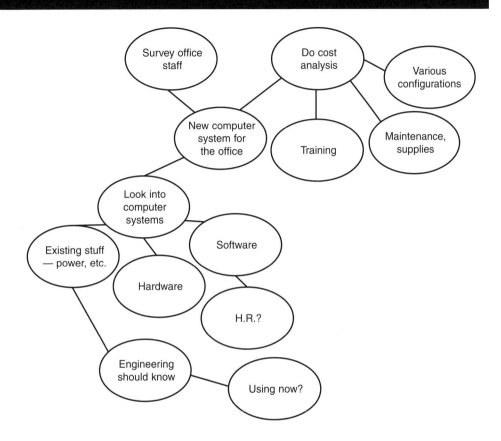

The author's next idea was to look into the various computer systems. From that, the ideas came to consider software, hardware and the existing use of facilities. You can follow the lines to see where the train of thought went.

Then the author thought of a survey of the office staff.

This is very different from what you are used to doing in the traditional outline method, but remember, the clustering method is faster and easier and works *with*, not *against*, your brain!

Organizing Your Cluster

Once you have your ideas captured on paper, you can then organize them into a format that will be the basis of your writing. In essence, you're creating a traditional outline right on your sheet of cluster ideas.

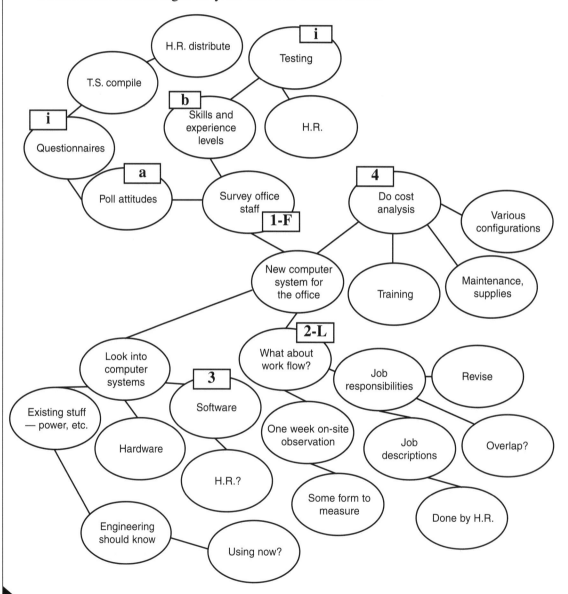

Analyze your cluster and decide which idea is the most important. Put a "1" next to it. Then put a "2" beside the second most important idea and so on. Under each idea, label the subheadings, "a, b, c," etc. You can go another level down with "i, ii, iii," etc., and then to "1, 2, 3," and so on. Now you have an outline.

Here's a tip: Put an "F" next to your first idea and an "L" by your second most important idea. That will remind you to write the most important idea in the first paragraph and the next most important idea in the last paragraph. Why? Because people generally remember best the first thing they read and the last thing they read! By arranging your ideas in this way, you're making sure that your readers remember the most important things in your document.

Most of the time, you'll be able to write directly from the cluster, but if you have a lot of scribbles and changes, then form the cluster into a traditional outline to make your writing task easier. Whichever way you choose, you're now ready to move to the next step — freewriting.

The management has decided to reorganize job roles and descriptions as part of a new realignment process. Employees in the organization have been asked to submit a memo outlining everything they do in a day, regardless of what their job descriptions say. They've also been asked to assign priorities to each task and indicate which tasks are related. You can prepare to write this memo by using the cluster method. Think about your job. Write down everything you do in a day. When you're finished, assign priorities (marking ideas 1, 2, 3, and so on) and show relationships. You'll find that the lines you've drawn from one idea to another will help you do this.

My job

Reflections

Reflections

6 FREEWRITING — THE METHOD

Most people will agree that the hardest thing about writing is just getting started — getting those first words onto the computer screen or onto that blank piece of paper! If you suffer from writing paralysis due to worrying where to start and how to say it, wondering if your grammar is correct or your spelling is right, feeling concerned about getting just the right word for what you want to say — then say goodbye to those writing blues! Freewriting is the business communicator's liberator.

The technique is simple. Just write. That's it. Nothing else. But that means that you are just writing, not analyzing the spelling and grammar, not searching for the perfect word, not concerning yourself with punctuation or syntax or even style. Learn how to do this, and you'll be amazed at how easy a task writing becomes.

Again, like clustering, you'll be working with your brain and not against it. You'll allow that right, imaginative side of the brain to spill out ideas and words without getting the left brain involved in analyzing the correctness of what you've written. Here's how to do it.

1. **Set a time limit.** Give yourself five minutes to begin with. You can increase the length of this time as you become adept at the technique of freewriting.

2. **Start writing.** Look at your cluster or outline. Choose which idea you want to begin with. It doesn't have to be #1 on the outline. You can go back and rearrange later. Then start writing.

3. **Write nonstop.** This is the hardest step of all because you'll be fighting your own tendency to edit as you write. Just do it. Spelling doesn't count. Neither does grammar, punctuation nor vocabulary. Penmanship isn't an issue, nor is fancy keyboarding. Don't worry about finding just the right word — substitute any word or leave a space. You'll come back later and find just that right word when you edit. Resist that impulse to edit, no matter what. If you can't think of what to say, write down, "I can't think of what to say right now … " and keep going.

4. **Let your mind go.** Allow your right brain to pour out the ideas without any censoring from the left brain. Once you've experienced the freedom of freewriting, you'll never go back to the old, labor-intensive, time-consuming method of combined writing/editing.

That's it — that's all there is to freewriting, but you will find that this method is an incredible way to produce fresh, powerful writing on any subject, anytime.

Using your cluster from the previous chapter, freewrite your memo. Remember, just start writing from any point in the cluster. Write for about five minutes. Then take a short break, and when you're ready, write some more.

Reflections

7 REWRITING — GRAMMAR AND NOUNS

"Words are, of course, the most powerful drug used by mankind."

— Rudyard Kipling

Now it's time to edit your freewritten work. It may seem like a daunting task, but if you approach it in a logical, sequential manner (a favorite of that left brain, which you'll use for editing), you'll find that you can feel confident that you've covered all the bases. Start with grammar, punctuation and spelling.

A Logical Progression

Let's look at a logical progression for your grammar editing. The easiest way to do this is to picture a set of building blocks.

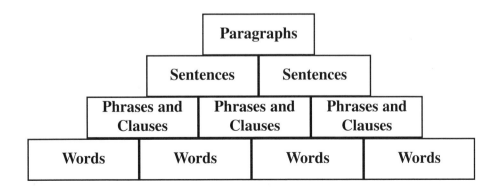

Looking at the pyramid, you can see that words are the foundation stones, followed by groups of words (phrases and clauses), followed by formal groups of words (sentences), and finally, by groups of sentences (paragraphs). This is the logical progression that you can use to edit your work.

The Words: Starting With Nouns

There are two main classes of words to deal with in editing: nouns and verbs. Begin with the nouns.

Nouns are words that name persons, places or things (objects, events, concepts).

Persons	Places	Things (Objects, Events, Concepts)		
worker	office	desk	picnic	freedom
woman	city	window	meeting	equality
child	beach	chair	skiing	liberty

Common, Proper and Collective Nouns

Common nouns refer to a general category or class of persons, places or things. Proper nouns name a particular person, place or thing. You must use a capital for proper nouns. Collective nouns name a group or unit and can be singular or plural.

Common Nouns	Proper Nouns	Collective Nouns
typist	Jack Bartell	staff
meeting	Housewares Show	team
town	Altoona	management

Note: You don't have to use a capital if a common noun is used with a proper noun, e.g., *Xerox copier* or *IBM computer*.

Count Nouns and Mass Nouns

Another distinction to be made among nouns is that of count nouns vs. mass nouns. Count nouns are those that name things that can be counted, such as *dogs*, *beans*, *companies* and *persons*. Mass nouns name substances that cannot be counted, such as *milk*, *sand*, *hair* and *applesauce*. Here are a few categories of mass nouns:

- Groups of similar items making up "wholes" — clothing, luggage, etc.

- Abstractions — truth, fun, peace, etc.

- Liquids

- Gases

- Particles or grains

- Sports, games, activities

- Languages

- Fields of study

- Events in nature — electricity, moonlight, thunder, etc.

Bear in mind that count nouns, when used as the subjects of sentences, always take the singular form of the verb.

Plural Nouns

You can make plurals in various ways. Most nouns form the plural by adding *s* to the singular form, e.g., *one ball*, *three balls*. However, due to the inconsistencies of the English language, plurals can be formed in many other ways.

Here are a couple of examples:

"Embargoes on the importing of pianos were discussed at the meeting."

(Note: The plural of embargo adds *es* while the plural of piano only adds *s,* although both words have the same ending.)

"Attorneys for the steel companies were consulted about the merger."

(Note: Both *attorney* and *company* end in *y*, but their plural forms are different.)

In many cases, you'll need to check for the correct plural form of the word you want. Always in grammar — if in doubt, check it out! However, there are four common plural problems that business writers face:

1. Plurals of names

Most common nouns form the plural by adding *s* to the singular form — *book, books*; *letter, letters*. However, common nouns ending in *s*, *sh*, *ch*, *x* and *z* form their plurals by adding *es* to the singular form.

Singular	Plural	Singular	Plural
lens	lenses	tax	taxes
brush	brushes	topaz	topazes
bench	benches		

Few writers make errors using *s* or *es* to form the plurals of common nouns. If you understand that the plurals of proper nouns or names are formed in exactly the same way, you'll make few errors when writing plurals of names.

Singular	*Plural*	*Singular*	*Plural*
farmer	farmers	Palmer	the Palmers
carton	cartons	Barton	the Bartons
brass	brasses	Ellis	the Ellises
dish	dishes	Walsh	the Walshes
branch	branches	Stritch	the Stritches
fox	foxes	Wilcox	the Wilcoxes
chintz	chintzes	Schlitz	the Schlitzes

2. Plurals of titles with names

When a title accompanies a name, make either the name or the title plural. Never make both the name and the title plural.

Singular	*Plural*
Mr. Carlin	*Messrs.* Carlin (*Messrs.* is from the French) or the two Mr. Carlins
Mrs. Fort	*Mmes.* Fort or the Mrs. Forts
Miss York	*Misses* York or the two Miss Yorks
Professor Weber	*Professors* Weber or the Professor Webers

3. Plurals with apostrophes

Over the years, grammar usage has dictated some changes in forming plurals with apostrophes. Here are four simple guidelines:

a) Use only lowercase *s* with capitals.

   "He sent several SOSs."

b) To form plurals of both uppercase and lowercase letters, add an apostrophe and *s*.

"I'm expecting to receive C.O.D's today by courier."

c) Form the plurals of numerals by adding an *s*.

"The temperature is in the 80s today."

d) Use (or don't use) an apostrophe and *s* if the plural form might be difficult to read or easily misread.

"Her g's and f's are poorly written."

"Try not to give the learner too many don'ts."

4. Plurals with compound nouns

A compound noun is a noun consisting of two or more words. It may be hyphenated or not. The rule to remember is this: The plural of a compound is formed with the most important or main word.

chief of police	*chiefs* of police
editor in chief	*editors* in chief
major general	major *generals*
personnel manager	personnel *managers*
son-in-law	*sons*-in-law

There are some instances when you'll want to be alert to plural problems. During your editing process, be sure to check out the following:

1. Plurals of nouns ending in y

a. Preceded by a consonant, change the *y* to *i* and add *es*.

supply   supplies

b. Preceded by a vowel (*a, e, i, o, u*), just add *s*.

valley   valleys

   c. Proper names ending in *y,* simply add *s.*

      Mary   three Marys

2. Plurals of nouns ending in *o*

   a. If the *o* is preceded by a vowel, add *s* to make it plural.

      studio   studios

   b. Here's the problem: Some nouns ending in *o* preceded by a consonant add *s* for plural and some add *es.* Check your dictionary if you're not sure.

      piano   pianos

      potato   potatoes

3. Plurals of nouns ending in *f* or *fe*

   a. Some nouns simply change the *f* to *v* and add *es.*

      shelf   shelves
      knife   knives

   b. Some nouns leave the *f* and add *s.*

      roof   roofs

The Gray Zone: What about a noun like data? Some writers think it should be a collective noun; others use it as a plural noun. Modern usage says you can use it as either a singular or a plural noun. Thus, you could correctly say, *"These data were compiled from several reports"* or *"The data is in from that study."*

Possessive Nouns

Today, there is a movement afoot to eliminate the use of the apostrophe in possessive cases. However, this has not met with universal approval, so for the time being, you must learn how to use the possessive case correctly in your business writing. There are three simple rules:

1. **For a plural word that ends in *s*, just add the apostrophe.**

   "The boys' lockers were empty."

   "Ladies' clothing is on sale today."

   Note: The plural forms of both *boys* and *ladies* end in *s*.

2. **For a word that does not end in the plural *s*, just add an apostrophe and *s*.**

   "The child's request was granted."   (Singular)

   "The children's request was granted." (Plural)

   Note: Neither *child* (singular) nor *children* (plural) ends in *s*.

3. **For a singular word ending in *s* that has an added syllable when its possessive form is pronounced, add an apostrophe and *s*.**

   "The actress's behavior was outrageous."

   "The witness's testimony was incorrect."

   Note: It takes an extra syllable to say the possessive forms *actress-sez* and *witness-sez*.

Quick Tip! One of the difficulties faced by business writers is determining which word should get the apostrophe in the possessive form. Here's an easy way to make that determination. Just say what is owned, followed by "of the" and then the ownership word. In the examples above, you would say, *"the request of the children"* or *"the lockers of the boys"* or *"the testimony of the witness."* In each case, it becomes easily clear which word will need to be made possessive. The ownership word is always made possessive.

Here are four possessive situations to watch for in your editing. They call for extra vigilance on your part.

1. **Possessive of a compound noun**

   The last word in a compound noun is the one that takes the possessive.

   "My sisters-in-law's families are coming for supper."

   Note: The compound noun *sisters-in-law* is a plural one. (Remember that the plural is always on the most important word.) To determine how to make it possessive, use the Quick Tip and say, "The families of my sisters-in-law." The possessive word is law — the last word in the compound. It doesn't end in *s* so just add an apostrophe and *s*, as the rules above for possessives tell you to do. Although this looks and sounds complicated, it isn't if you take the time to work it through using the information you already have.

2. **Joint or separate ownership**

   Show joint ownership by using the apostrophe with the last member of the combination.

   "Jane and Sue's mother is a college professor."

   Note: Jane and Sue have the same mother.

   Show separate ownership by using an apostrophe with each member of the combination.

   "Jane's, Sue's and Mary's mothers are coming for graduation."

   Note: All three have separate mothers.

3. Appositives showing possession

Don't let the word *appositive* throw you. It simply means "a phrase which explains or gives additional information." If you have an appositive, the words in the phrase show possession.

"That is Miss Downy, the file clerk's, responsibility."

Note: The appositive "the file clerk" gives you additional information.

4. Possessive case before a gerund

A gerund is a verb form ending in *ing* that is used as a noun. For example, *"Walking* to work is beneficial to your health." Any noun (or pronoun) that precedes a gerund must have the possessive form.

"Did Ray's checking of your returns help you?"

"We would appreciate your returning the sales slip with your purchase."

Quick Tip! If you're not sure of a possessive form, you can always change it around and make a sentence that doesn't need the possessive form. In the appositive example above, you could write, *"Miss Downy, the file clerk, has that responsibility."* In other examples, you could say, *"The mother of Jane and Sue is a college professor."* You can even do this with those pesky gerunds — *"Did the checking of your returns by Ray help you?"*

You won't need to worry about possessive ever again!

Warning: Here is one last note on possessives. In formal writing, inanimate objects do not take the possessive. In other words, a house cannot own a door. Instead of *"The house's door is painted red,"* the preferred form is *"The house door is painted red."* This includes such things as a company or an organization. Rather than *"The company's policy states ... ,"* write, *"The company policy states ... "*

Before you put a noun into a possessive case, ask yourself, "Is this a living, breathing creature?" If the answer is no, avoid the possessive case.

Remember, you can avoid this problem, too, if you simply rewrite the sentence to eliminate all possessives. You could write, *"The door of the house is painted red." "The policy of the company states ... "*

How proficient are you with the use of nouns? Find and correct the seven errors in the following piece of business writing.

The facultys of all three schools will attend the conference.

However, the Doctors Smiths have not yet replied to our invitation.

We're hoping that the company's policys will not be violated if we

ask the Jones's if they can come also. The conference's board is

trying to include as many former editors and editors-in-chiefs as

they can to round out the discussions. So far, only three RSVP's

have been returned.

Corrections:
The **faculty** of all three schools will attend the conference. However, the Doctors **Smith** have not yet replied to our invitation. We're hoping that the **company policies** will not be violated if we ask the **Joneses** if they can come also. The **conference board** is trying to include as many editors and editors-in-**chief** as they can to round out the discussions. So far, only three **RSVPs** have been returned.

Reflections
Reflections

8 REWRITING — GRAMMAR AND PRONOUNS

"'When I use a word,' Humpty Dumpty said in rather a scornful tone, 'it means just what I choose it to mean — neither more nor less.'"

— Lewis Carroll

Another group of words that form the foundation of your writing is pronouns. Pronouns simply take the place of nouns. It would be pretty tiresome for your reader if you wrote something like this: *"Bloggs Brothers wants Mrs. Jones to know that Bloggs Brothers has Mrs. Jones' order ready, and Mrs. Jones can pick the order up from Bloggs Brothers' warehouse on Saturday."*

If you substitute pronouns, the sentence would read, *"We want you to know that we have your order ready, and you can pick it up from our warehouse on Saturday."*

Pronouns make your writing more readable and more personal for the reader. They give your writing clarity and a businesslike tone. However, you must use them properly!

Pronoun Case

Suppose the letters you received in today's mail contained the following sentences:

"Please let any of our officers or myself know when you hear from him."

"The higher price will affect we retailers' sales projections."

"You can depend on John and I to back up your proposal."

Each of these sentences will give you a negative impression of that writer because the pronouns have been used incorrectly.

Case describes the form of a noun or a pronoun and indicates its relation to other words in the sentence. There are three cases:

1. Nominative or subjective

2. Accusative or objective

3. Possessive

A pronoun form called the "reflexive" or "intensive" is also used and is always in the objective case.

Here's a chart that will show you the personal pronouns (those pronouns that take the place of persons) in these four forms:

Person	Case	Singular	Plural
First:	subjective	I	we
	objective	me	us
	possessive	my/mine	our/ours
	(reflexive)	myself	ourselves
Second:	subjective	you	you
	objective	you	you
	possessive	your/yours	your/yours
	(reflexive)	yourself	yourselves
Third:	subjective	he/she/it	they
	objective	him/her/it	them
	possessive	his/her/hers/its	their/theirs
	(reflexive)	himself/herself/ itself	themselves

1. Nominative or subjective case

There are only three rules that you need to be aware of in order to use pronouns correctly in the subjective case.

a) Subject of a verb: If the pronoun is the subject of the verb in a sentence, use the subjective case. This is an easy one for you to remember because it sounds correct.

"I will go to the bank."

Note: You'd probably feel uncomfortable with *"Me will go to the bank,"* because it doesn't sound right.

b) Objective complement with a "being" verb: A *being* verb is a form of the verb "to be" and includes *is, am, are, was, were, has been* and *have been*. The problem is that it often doesn't sound right because the objective pronoun is used so often in our day-to-day conversations.

"If I were (he? him?), I would correct the error."

Note: *Were* is a being verb, so you'll need to use the form *he*, even if it sounds odd to you.

c) Complements the infinitive "to be": In this case, the infinitive form of the verb is being used, and the infinitive of the "being" verb is followed by the nominative case. But there's a problem: Even though use of the word *I* obeys the strictest rules of grammarians, general and business usage prefers *me*.

"Who would ever wish to be (I? me?)?"

"In the dark, she thought Harry to be (I? me?)."

2. Objective case

The easiest way to know when to use the objective case of a pronoun is to realize that if it doesn't meet one of the three rules for the nominative/subjective case, then it must be objective! That's all you need to do.

3. Possessive case

Unlike possessive nouns, possessive pronouns do not take an apostrophe. As you can see from the chart, possessive pronouns have their own possessive form. One common error in this regard involves the possessive pronoun *its*. Never use an apostrophe when you are using *its* as a possessive. Remember, the word *it's* ALWAYS means IT IS!

A major exception important to business writing is the pronoun *one*. That is the only pronoun that takes an apostrophe:

"One must stick to one's principles."

4. Reflexive/intensive forms

Myself, yourself, himself, herself, itself, ourselves, yourselves and *themselves* are the pronouns ending in *self*. These pronouns are often mistakenly used in place of the nominative or objective case form of a personal pronoun. For example, in the sentence, *"Mrs. Cole and myself will be happy to accept your invitation,"* the writer is unsure about *me* or *I* and tries to substitute *myself*. This is not good practice in business writing. There are two ways to use these pronouns:

a) Intensive use: to intensify or emphasize the meaning of a statement.

"I myself did not agree with the vote."

b) To reflect some noun or pronoun that has already been named.

"I could not bring myself to look at the accident."

Note: *Myself* reflects back to *I.*

Quick Tip! If you aren't sure about *myself,* try this trick. Substitute the word *I* or *me,* and if it can be correctly substituted, eliminate the *myself.* For example, *"I myself did not agree with the vote."* You can't correctly substitute *"I (I, me) did not agree with the vote."* However, in our earlier example, *"Mrs. Cole and (I, me) will be happy to accept your invitation,"* you can correctly substitute *I,* and so *myself* is incorrect in this instance.

Pronoun Challenges

1. Noun-pronoun agreement

A pronoun must always refer to a word called its antecedent. You must make sure that a pronoun refers to a specific antecedent. More importantly, that pronoun must agree with its antecedent in person, gender and number.

"When the operator exits the program, you must use the proper sequence."

Note: You can correct this in two ways: Make the antecedent plural — *operators* — and then use *they* as the pronoun. Or use *he or she* as the joint pronoun since the gender of the operator isn't known.

"Each December, the company publishes their report."

Note: *Company* is singular and requires a singular pronoun — the third person, possessive form *its.* (No apostrophe — remember?)

2. Who or whom?

Even experienced writers confuse *who* or *whom*. Rather than worrying about how to do it correctly by the book, use this simple tip.

Quick Tip! Substitute *he* or *him* for *who* or *whom*. If *he* is correct, use *who*. If *him* is correct, use *whom*. Memory help: Both *him* and *whom* end in *m*. That's all there is to it — the end of your who/whom woes!

"I can tell (who/whom) is coming down the road." Use substitution: *"I can tell (he/him) is coming down the road."* Correct substitution is *" … he is coming down the road."* Therefore, use *who* in this sentence.

"Give the package to (whoever, whomever) comes to the door." Substitute *he* or *him*: *"Give the package to him … ."* Thus, in this sentence, *whomever* is correct.

3. Relative pronouns: who, that, which

Who always refers to human beings.

"The man who was here yesterday called again today."

That can refer to a person but better to an object.

"The vase that sat on the table was broken."

Which always refers to an object, never a person.

"The game which the children played most often was Snap."

4. Indefinite pronouns

These are a group of pronouns such as *everybody, nobody, anybody somebody, none, each*. The question that plagues most business writers is whether these are singular or plural forms. Use the quick tip to help you make the right decision.

Quick Tip! Put the word *one* between the two parts of an indefinite pronoun or directly after the pronoun. This will tell you that these words are singular in nature and refer to only one person in the group.

"Everybody (is, are) going on the field trip." Say to yourself, *"Every one body is going on the field trip."* Correct verb: *is*.

"Each of the consultants (is, are) paid commission." Say to yourself, *"Each one of the consultants is paid commission."* Correct verb: *is*.

Note: If using the pronoun *none* (a contraction of *not one*), it already has one in it to remind you that it is singular.

You received this memo in the interoffice mail this morning. Can you find and correct the seven pronoun errors in it?

I'm not sure who to send this memo to, but I figured you were the best one to get it. Everybody in the field divisions are talking about the new plans for reorganization, and their all afraid that its going to make a mess of their jobs. Do you know anyone whom might be able to help give those a better idea of what's going on, instead of me going on and on about it as I try to explain it to the others?

Corrections:
I'm not sure **whom** to send this memo to (to whom to send this memo), but I figured you were the best one to get it. **People** in the field divisions are talking about the new plans for reorganization, and **they're** all afraid that **it's** going to make a mess of their jobs. Do you know anyone **who** might be able to help give **them** a better idea of what's going on, instead of **my** going on and on about it as I try to explain it to others?

Reflections

9 REWRITING — GRAMMAR AND VERBS

"The verbs in English are a fright. How can we learn to read and write? Today we speak, but first we spoke. Some faucets leak, but never loke. Today we write, but first we wrote. We bite our tongues, but never bote."

— Richard Lederer

To convey meaning in your business correspondence, you must be comfortable in using correct verbs and verb forms. A verb is a word that asserts or assumes:

- Action — The boy *ran* home.

- A condition — The boy *felt* excited.

- A state of being — The boy *is* sick.

All verbs have two form divisions — forms which can be used as the predicate (the verb that states the action of the subject) of the sentence and three forms which cannot be used as a predicate without a helping form called an "auxiliary" or a "modal." Those three forms are the infinitive — often preceded by the word *to* (*to be*, *to go*, *to navigate*, etc.); the present participle — the form ending with *-ing*; and the past participle — the form usually ending with *-ed* but sometimes with *-en*. You would not want to write:

- *"I to use the office copier."*

- *"We having an office party."*

- *"We taken the computer to be repaired."*

For the infinitive, you always use a modal, such as *want*, *need*, *like*, etc.

"I need to use the office copier."

For the present participle, you normally use as the auxiliary a form of the verb "to be."

"We are having an office party."

For the past participle, you normally use as the auxiliary a form of the verb "to have."

"We have taken the computer to be repaired."

The exception to the above is the passive voice, in which the verb "to be" is used with the past participle. The passive voice will be discussed below.

The forms that can be used as the predicate are the conjugated forms. Three sample conjugations are shown below.

Present Tense

	To Be (inf.)	To Go (inf.)	To Take (inf.)
Singular			
First person:	I am	I go	I take
Second person:	You are	You go	You take
Third person:	She/he/it is	He/she/it goes	It/she/he takes
Plural			
First person:	We are	We go	We take
Second person:	You are	You go	You take
Third person:	They are	They go	They take

Past Tense

	To Be (inf.)	To Go (inf.)	To Take (inf.)
Singular			
First person:	I was	I went	I took
Second person:	You were	You went	You took
Third person:	He was	She went	It took
Plural			
First person:	We were	We went	We took
Second person:	You were	You went	You took
Third person:	They were	They went	They took
Present participle	Being	Going	Taking
Past participle	Been	Gone	Taken

And that's how you conjugate a verb! Notice that the conjugated forms all look alike — though they are NOT alike — except for the third person singular form, which has an *s* on the end. Here's another tip: Between the third person singular subject and the verb of your sentence, you get only one *s*; if the subject is singular, the *s* goes on the end of the verb:

> *"The boy leaves."*

If the subject is plural, the *s* goes on the end of the noun:

> *"The boys leave."*

Regular and Irregular Verbs

Verbs are classified as regular or irregular, depending on the way their principal parts are formed. These principal parts form the tense of a verb:

- Past tense — The boy *walked* home.

- Present tense — The boy *walks* home.

- Future tense — The boy *will walk* home.

A regular verb forms the past tense and the past participle (the form of verb that links with *have*, *has* or *had*) by adding *ed*. An irregular verb often has a completely different form for the past tense and past participle.

- Regular verb — I call. I called. I have been called.

- Irregular verb — I ride. I rode. I have ridden.

You'll need to either memorize or always check the irregular verbs to make sure you're using the proper form.

Here's a list of the main irregular verbs that you're likely to need and their tenses. Always refer to this list if you're using a helper verb with your main verb.

Base Form	Past Tense	Past Participle	Present Participle
be	was	been	being
begin	began	begun	beginning
bite	bit	bit/bitten	biting
blow	blew	blown	blowing
break	broke	broken	breaking
bring	brought	brought	bringing
burst	burst	burst	bursting
buy	bought	bought	buying
catch	caught	caught	catching
come	came	come	coming
do	did	done	doing
draw	drew	drawn	drawing
drink	drank	drunk	drinking
drive	drove	driven	driving

Base Form	Past Tense	Past Participle	Present Participle
eat	ate	eaten	eating
fall	fell	fallen	falling
fight	fought	fought	fighting
flee	fled	fled	fleeing
fly	flew	flown	flying
forget	forgot	forgotten	forgetting
get	got	got/gotten	getting
give	gave	given	giving
go	went	gone	going
grow	grew	grown	growing
hang	hung	hung	hanging
hide	hid	hidden	hiding
know	knew	known	knowing
lay	laid	laid	laying
leave	left	left	leaving
lend	lent	lent	lending
lie	lay	lain	lying
lose	lost	lost	losing
pay	paid	paid	paying
ride	rode	ridden	riding
ring	rang	rung	ringing
rise	rose	risen	rising
run	ran	run	running
see	saw	seen	seeing
set	set	set	setting
shake	shook	shaken	shaking
shine	shone	shone	shining
shrink	shrank/shrunk	shrunk/shrunken	shrinking
sit	sat	sat	sitting
speak	spoke	spoken	speaking
steal	stole	stolen	stealing
strike	struck	struck/stricken	striking
take	took	taken	taking
tear	tore	torn	tearing
throw	threw	thrown	throwing
wear	wore	worn	wearing
write	wrote	written	writing

Verb Conundrums — Which to Use?

The business writer is often faced with a choice of words, both of which may sound right. Here are some of the more common business verbs you'll use.

1. **Lend, loan**

   Generally speaking, *lend* is a verb and *loan* is a noun.

   "The bank will loan you the money." According to the dictionary, this usage is not incorrect; however, the preferred usage is *"The bank will lend you the money if you ask the bank for a loan."*

2. **Lie, lay; set, set; rise, raise**

   Here they are in an easy table form to use. Apply the Quick Tip that follows, and this will no longer be one of your verb conundrums.

Present	Past	Past Participle	Present Participle	Infinitive
lie	lay	lain	lying	to lie
lay	laid	laid	laying	to lay
sit	sat	sat	sitting	to sit
set	set	set	setting	to set
rise	rose	risen	rising	to rise
raise	raised	raised	raising	to raise

Quick Tip! Notice that there is an *i* or an *i* sound in the present form of one member of each pair of verbs. These *i* verbs are *lie, sit* and *rise*. You'll use these and all forms of the verb when the question "what" or "whom" can't be answered after the verb.

"I (lie/lay) down." Ask yourself, "I lie/lay what or whom down?" In this case, the answer to the question is "nothing" so use the *i* form of the verb. *"I lie down."*

Note: This is a puzzle in itself, since using *lie* here indicates the present tense of the verb. But the past tense would be *"I lay down."*

"I lie/lay the book down." Ask yourself, *"I lie/lay what or whom down?" The answer to the question is "the book," so use the form of the verb without the *i*. *"I lay the book down."* This is the present tense. The past tense in this case would be *"I laid the book down."*

3. **Affect, effect**

The verb *affect* means "to influence."

"How did the new system affect the office?"

The verb *effect* means "to cause" or "to bring about."

"The new manager intends to effect major changes here."

The noun *effect* refers to whatever has been affected or effected.

"What was the effect of the new system on the office?"

The noun *affect* is a technical term and will rarely if ever be used in your business writing unless you work for a psychologist.

4. **A short list of other verbs often confused with sound-alike words:**

- **Accept** — to take; to receive
- **Except** (prep.) — exclude

- **Advice** (noun) — suggestion
- **Advise** — to counsel; to inform

- **Complement** — to complete or fulfill
- **Compliment** — to say nice things

- **Council** (noun) — an assembly
- **Counsel** — to give advice

- **Envelop** — to surround; to enclose
- **Envelope** (noun) — a container

- **Loose** (adj.) — unfastened
- **Lose** — to mislay

- **Passed** — past tense of *to pass*
- **Past** (noun) — time before

- **Precede** — to go or come before or in front of
- **Proceed** — to move forward

Active vs. Passive Voice

Verbs can be in either the active or the passive voice. Either one is acceptable for business writing, but business writers tend to use the passive voice to excess. This may create writing that is dull, impersonal and lacking in interest. It also gives rise to certain types of errors that can embarrass you or your employer or, even worse, cost money!

What's the difference between active and passive voice? Generally speaking, if you use a form of the verb *to be* (*am, are, is, was, were,* etc.), combined with the past participle form of the main verb in the sentence, you're using the passive voice of the verb. The following example uses the active voice.

> *"The messenger collected the mail."*

Note that in the preceding sentence the verb directs an action toward an object. The following example uses the passive voice, and the verb directs the action toward the subject.

> *"The mail was collected by the messenger."*

Note: You can see that in this example, a form of the verb *to be* is used with the past participle *collected*. The *mail*, as the subject of the verb, is not doing anything but is merely being acted upon. Contrast this with the active voice of the same example.

If you are a business writer who wants to make your work more personal, more lively and more interesting, try to avoid the passive form of verbs whenever possible. Certainly, be careful to avoid more than two passive sentences in a row. Here are some more examples of how the active voice livens up the information:

> *"The package was delivered by us."*

> vs. *"We delivered the package."*

> *"The message has been checked."*

vs. *"Mr. Smith checked his message."*

"It was brought to my attention that ... "

vs. *"I learned that ... "*

Another form that you should know about is the "get passive."

"The package got delivered on time."

Some Common Problems With Verbs

1. The dangling participle

Since we have just been discussing the passive voice, let's begin with one of the major problems that arises from the use of this form. Take a look at a sentence introduced by a "participial phrase" — a phrase characterized by a verb ending with *-ing*.

"Having started early, the messenger delivered the package on time."

In a sentence of this type, the reader expects the introductory phrase to modify the first available noun in the main part of the sentence. In this case the noun is *messenger*, and the reader knows that it is the messenger who started early. However, since the package is more important here, why not make the sentence passive so as to emphasize the package — not the messenger.

"Having started early, the package was delivered on time by the messenger."

Now the reader is first confused, then irritated at having to recalculate the sentence, and finally amused at the apparent fact that it was the *package* that started early! Suppose now that you decide to remove the messenger from the sentence altogether, since only the package really matters, so you write:

"Having started early, the package was delivered on time."

You now have a full-grown dangling modifier! A modifier with nothing to modify. Your remedy? Either go back to your first overly long but perfectly correct sentence or remove the unnecessary modifier.

2. The split infinitive

You may have heard about split infinitives and how "incorrect" they are. But, do you even know what they are? As shown above, an infinitive is a form of verb in which the word *to* is used.

to run, to shout, to sing, to come

Older grammar practices say that you cannot split an infinitive form of a verb, that is, put something between *to* and the verb.

to quickly run, to loudly shout, to happily sing, to slowly come

---

The Gray Zone: Although in the past, splitting infinitives was considered a major grammatical error, current usage is not so strict. In fact, the opening lines of one of the most well-known motion-picture series in the world begins with a split infinitive: *"To boldly go where no one has gone before …"* It's unlikely that anyone will fault you — or even notice it — if you do split an infinitive in your business writing but keep in mind that there are some readers for whom grammar rules may never be broken.

You are reviewing applications for a new secretary. This was the body of a cover letter from one of the applicants. Can you find and correct the seven verb errors in it?

In reference to Position #453

My years of experience as a clerk typist in the Claims Department

should be of help to this position. To quickly work on complex

statements are one of my strengths. I also have went to court a

number of times to efficiently help my boss with some of his cases.

I has some experience in detective work, too. My boss would get

me to set and wait for some of the deadbeats and catch them if they

was lying about their claim …

Corrections:
My years of experience as a clerk typist in the Claims Department should be of help to this position. **To work quickly** on complex statements **is** one of my strengths. I also have **gone** to court a number of times **to help my boss efficiently** with some of his cases. **I have** some experience in detective work, too. My boss would get me to **sit** and wait for some of the deadbeats and catch them if they **were** lying about their claim.

Reflections

10 REWRITING — GRAMMAR: ADJECTIVES AND ADVERBS

"In fact, words are well adapted for descriptions and arousing emotions, but for many kinds of precise thought other symbols are much better."

— J.B.S. Haldane

"This is the most unkindest cut of all … "

— Shakespeare

Adjectives — a Definition

Adjectives are words that describe, enhance, limit, or in some other way modify nouns and pronouns. You can easily identify adjectives because they answer any of three questions about the noun they modify: Which?, What kind of? or How many?

Quick Tip! Because you live in an advertising age, your readers have learned to ignore adjectives. The specific details about any subject — person, place, product, service or idea — are what grabs the reader's attention. Compare: *"The new computer has proven to be a cost-effective alternative to the old word processors"* with *"The RAM has cut our operating costs by 30 percent."* When you've finished the first draft of any writing, go back and circle the adjectives you've used. After each adjective, ask, "What did I mean by this word?" Take the first answer that comes to mind, cross out the adjective and put what you mean in its place.

You're probably comfortable with putting descriptive adjectives with your nouns and pronouns: the *beautiful* view, the *large* dog, the *horrible, tasteless* meal. Writing troubles multiply when you decide to compare various nouns.

Comparison of Adjectives

Most adjectives change their forms to express different degrees of quality. This is called comparison. There are three forms or degrees of adjective comparison:

- **Positive** — when the adjective is not compared to anything else.

- **Comparative** — when an adjective is compared to its positive degree.

- **Superlative** — when an adjective is the highest or lowest degree.

1. **The three forms of adjective comparison**

    a. Add *er* to the positive to form the comparative degree and *est* to the positive to form the superlative degree.

Positive	Comparative	Superlative
quick	quicker	quickest
happy	happier	happiest
late	later	latest

    b. Insert the word *more* or *less* before the positive to form the comparative degree and *most* or *least* before the positive to form the superlative degree.

Positive	Comparative	Superlative
Patient	more (less) patient	most (least) patient
punctual	more (less) punctual	most (least) punctual
responsible	more (less) responsible	most (least) responsible

c. Change the form of the word completely.

Positive	Comparative	Superlative
much, many	more	most
little	less	least
good	better	best
bad	worse	worst

2. How to select the right form of adjective comparison

- Adjectives of one syllable are compared by adding *er*, *est*.

- Adjectives of three or more syllables add *more*, *less*, *most*, *least*.

- Adjectives of two syllables can use either form.

  "Jane is the prettiest girl in the room." (Not *most pretty*)

  "The computer is more useful than the typewriter." (Not *usefuler*)

3. Modifying count nouns and mass nouns

Do not use the comparative adjectives *less* and *fewer* interchangeably. Use *less* with mass nouns and *fewer* with count nouns.

"They consumed fewer calories."

"The sugar substitute had less aftertaste."

4. Double comparison

As you can see from the quote from Shakespeare's *"Julius Caesar"* at the heading of this chapter, the double comparison has not always been considered incorrect but beware! Using two forms of comparison with the same adjective is now considered a grammar error.

"This is the fairest contract." (Not *most fairest*)

"The box has smoother edges." (Not *more smoother*)

The Gray Zone: Absolute adjectives are adjectives that cannot be compared because in the positive degree, they are already tops. For instance, if you have a *full* glass of water, you can't have a *fuller* glass. However, modern usage recognizes that you can compare these absolutes. *"Our encyclopedias are the most complete editions on the market."*

Compound Adjectives — to Hyphenate or Not to Hyphenate

Here is a quick rule for you to remember:

If the two adjectives form a single idea, they should be hyphenated.

- *fast-thinking executive*
- *pollution-conscious efforts*
- *part-time job*
- *past-due bill*
- *fund-raising efforts*

Adverbs — a Definition

Adverbs modify verbs, adjectives and other adverbs. They answer questions such as When? Where? How? How much? If? and Whether? Adverbs give additional information and describe an action or state of being in greater detail.

> *"She never leaves the office before I do."* (When?)

> *"I think they went upstairs."* (Where?)

> *"Please get this quickly."* (How?)

> *"I agree somewhat with your decision."* (How much?)

Most adverbs end in *ly*; some do not.

Adverb Confusion

1. When to use *ly* form

Not all verbs denote action. Verbs such as *seem*, *appear*, *look, sound*, *taste* and *smell* do not always express action. They are called linking verbs. Do not use the *ly* adverb form with a no-action verb.

"Don said that the coffee tasted strong."

"Barb felt bad when her suggestion was ignored."

However, if the verb is an action verb, then the *ly* ending is used with the adverb.

"Don tasted the coffee gingerly before he drank it."

"Barb felt stealthily in her purse for the keys."

2. Never, not

Never and *not* are both adverbs, but they shouldn't be used interchangeably for their meanings are quite different. *Never* means "not ever, at no time," while *not* is simply a word that expresses negation in a specific or immediate situation.

"Ms. Lyons said she did not receive your memo." (Not *she never received your memo*.)

However, if you queried Ms. Lyons a week later as to whether she had received the memo, she might write back:

"No, I never did receive your memo."

A high-credit company, upon receiving a dun for a late payment that it had already sent in, might well indignantly write back:

"We have never been late in interest payments."

3. Where, that

Use the word *that*, not *where*, after such expressions as *"I saw in the paper,"* etc.

"Did you read in the paper that our company is expanding?" (Not *read in the paper where … .*)

Adverb and Adjective Confusion

1. Sure, surely; real, really

When an adjective is needed, use *sure* or *real*. When an adverb is required, use *surely* or *really*.

"The boss was really angry this morning."

"That is real fur on her hat."

Quick Tip! If the word *very* or *certainly* can be substituted, use the same form of the word that also ends in *y: surely*, *really*. If it can't be substituted, use *sure* or *real*.

"The boss was certainly angry this morning." (Use *really*.)

"That is very fur on her hat." (Use *real*.)

2. **Good, well**

   Good is the adjective and *well* is the adverb, except when referring to health. If the question "How?" can be answered, use *well*; if the question "How?" cannot be answered, use *good*. Remember, though, that *well* is always used when speaking of health.

   "The new correspondent does good work."

   "The new correspondent works well." (Answers *How?*)

   "She isn't feeling well today."

3. **Most, almost**

   Most is an adjective, the superlative of *much* or *many*. *Almost* is an adverb, meaning "not quite" or "very nearly."

   "Most secretaries have transcribed almost all their dictation by three o'clock."

4. **Some, somewhat**

   Some is an adjective; *somewhat*, an adverb.

Quick Tip! Use *somewhat* if you can substitute the words *a little bit;* otherwise, use *some. "Mr. King was (some? somewhat?) doubtful about the plan."* You can substitute *a little bit*, so use the adverb *somewhat*.

Your boss returned this memo to you and told you there were seven glaring errors in it. Can you find and correct them?

The line change-over would have happened more quicker if we had known about the new improved discount products coming out in July. The old product line did appear strongly at the time, but subsequent factors changed the plans. The Sales Manager felt the old line really need a big boost to make it real competitive in the market. I know she would be some pleased with the results as we see them today.

Corrections:
The line **changeover** would have happened more **quickly** if we had known about the **newly** improved discount products coming out in July. The old product line did appear **strong** at the time, but subsequent factors changed the plans. The Sales Manager felt the old line really **needed** a big boost to make it **really** competitive in the market. I know she would be **somewhat** pleased with the results as we see them today.

Reflections

11 GRAMMAR — PHRASES AND CLAUSES (PREPOSITIONS AND CONJUNCTIONS)

"Words, like eyeglasses, blur everything that they do not make clearer."

— Joseph Joubert

"What did you bring that book that I didn't want to be read to out of up for?"

— 10-year-old

Phrases and Clauses — Definitions

A phrase is a group of words that doesn't have a subject or verb but gives meaning to the sentence. When a phrase begins with a preposition, it is referred to as a "prepositional phrase." A preposition is any one of a large number of adverbial particles used with a noun, which is called the "object of the preposition."

> *"The insurance agent runs his business from a computer that is located in his living room."*

This sentence contains two prepositional phrases: *from a computer* and *in his living room*. The two prepositions are *from* and *in*. The nouns *computer* and *living room* are the objects of the preposition.

Also in the sentence above, notice the last part, *" … that is located in his living room."* This portion of the sentence is called a "dependent clause" or a "subordinate clause."

Clauses have both a subject and a verb and often look like sentences. There are two kinds of clauses.

1. **Independent clause:** Contains both a subject and verb and can stand alone as a sentence.

   "I won't comment right now."

2. **Dependent (subordinate) clause:** Contains both subject and verb but can't stand alone as a sentence because it begins with a connecting word (conjunction) that indicates it needs more information to be complete.

   "As I am not familiar with that subject, ... "

   Note: This is a dependent clause not a complete sentence. It contains a subject *I* and a verb *am* but begins with a conjunction, *as*. To complete it, you might say, *"As I am not familiar with that subject, I won't comment right now."*

Independent Clauses	Dependent Clauses
She was hired today	when she was hired today
Each one of us called	why each one of us called
I'm five minutes late	because I'm five minutes late
The schedule is changed	how the schedule is changed

A complete sentence can contain both clauses and phrases.

"As I am not familiar with that subject, I won't comment right now."

- Dependent clause: *as I am not familiar with that subject*

- Prepositional phrase: *with that subject*

- Independent clause: *I won't comment right now*

The Overuse of Phrases

One of the first signs of insecure writers is the number of phrases they use to say what could be said in just a few words. Instead of writing *now* or *then*, these writers hang on to *at this point in time*. Not only do these phrases pad messages with unnecessary words, they are trite and dull. Eliminate as many clichés as you can. Here are a few to watch for in your writing.

Trite Phrase	Powerful Word
Prior to	Before
Upon that date	Then
At that point in time	Then
At this point in time	Now
In reference to	Regarding

Quick Tip! Here's some advice for handling prepositional phrases. Check your sentences for these:

- Two phrases in a row — no problem.

- Three in a row — think twice about it.

- Four or more in a row — always a disaster!

Prepositions

Prepositions begin phrases, but they are little words with plenty of power in your writing. If you use the wrong preposition, it can change the meaning of your sentence.

1. Agree with, agree to

Persons can agree with persons, who can in turn agree back with them; and things can agree with things, which can also have a reciprocal relationship.

"Don thinks it is a good policy to agree with the boss."

"A pronoun must agree with its antecedent."

However, the expression *agree to* means "to give consent" and is not a reciprocal relationship.

"Don won't agree to any policy in the report."

Moreover, in this sentence, *to* is connected to the verb *agree* and is not a preposition at all but an adverbial particle.

Sometimes, *agree to* is followed by a verb.

"Don won't agree to attend the seminar."

In this sentence, the *to* is an infinitive particle attached to *attend*. As you can see, the word *to* can be a confusing little dickens! (See end of this chapter.)

2. Angry with, angry at

Use *angry with* when the object of the preposition is a person who can get angry back at you; use *angry at* when the object is not a person.

"We were angry with the repairman for overcharging."

"We were angry at the poor service we received."

3. Part from, part with

Part from means "to take leave of"; *part with* means "to relinquish, to give up." *Part from* is generally used when the object of the preposition is a person; *part with* is used when the object is not a person.

"What time did you part from Kent?"

"How can you bear to part with your heirlooms?"

4. In regard to, with regard to, as regards

These three phrases are equally correct, but *regards* cannot be used with *in* or *with*. Whenever *regards*, which ends in *s*, is used, then use *as*, which also ends in *s*. Better yet, simply use the word *regarding* or *as to*.

"This is the third time we've notified you in regard to your error."

"As regards our indemnity on the matter, you'll have to speak to our lawyer."

5. Different from, identical with, retroactive to

You'll need to memorize the correct prepositions to be used after *different*, *identical* and *retroactive*.

"Do you have samples different from these?" (Not *different than*)

"Check to see whether your total is identical with Peter's." (Not *identical to*)

"Is your pay increase retroactive to May?" (Not *retroactive from*)

Preposition Pitfalls

Here are some commonly used prepositions that you may find cause you some difficulties. If in doubt, always look the word up or rewrite the sentence.

1. **Between, among**

   Between is commonly used when referring to two persons, places or things; *among* refers to more than two.

   "We can't choose between Larry and Jack."

   "We have to choose among the seven contestants."

   The preposition *between* has its own problem that you should be aware of. Unlike other prepositions, *between* will always have two objects. If one or both of these objects are pronouns, the pronouns will always be in the objective case. Many people were told as children, *"Don't say 'George and ME are going to the store' — always say 'George and I!'"* As a result, they think that any time "George" gets into the sentence, it must be as "George and I." These are the people — are you among them? — who think it correct to say, "between George and I." (They are equally liable to say something like "Please do this for George and I.") If you are tempted to do this — don't! After all, would you say, "for I"? Of course not! So when you have a compound object, one of which is a pronoun, temporarily remove the one that is not a pronoun. Then you will know which pronoun to use. After that, put "George" back in. The problem is that you can't do that with *between*. So just remember that after *between*, you ALWAYS use the objective case pronoun — *me, him, her, them.*

   "There is some tension between my boss and me."

   "I can't choose between Mary and her or between George and him."

   "Between them and the other personnel, they got the job done."

2. **Beside, besides**

   Beside means "by the side of"; *besides* means "in addition to."

   "I was seated beside the guest of honor."

   "How many others besides you have the blue model?"

3. **Inside, outside**

   The preposition *of* is not used after *inside* or *outside*. If you're referring to time, use *within*, not *inside of.*

   "Her desk is just inside the reception area."

   "The project has to be done within a week." (Not *inside of*)

4. **Should of**

   Of is a preposition; *have* is a verb. Don't fall into the common trap of saying *should of* when you mean *should have.*

   "He should have called her today." (Not *should of*)

5. **Where … at, where … to**

   The use of *at* or *to* with *where* is illiterate!

   "Do you know where he is?" (Not *where he is at!*)

   "Where did she go?" (Not *go to!*)

The Gray Zone: What about ending sentences with prepositions? Avoid it where possible but don't create an awkward, unnatural sentence simply to avoid it. It has always been common usage that questions can end with prepositions, such as, *"What are you going there for?"* rather than *"For what are you going there?"* But why do either when you can say, *"Why are you going there?"*

6. Prepositions vs. adverbial particles

Caution — those little words are not always prepositions! Sometimes, instead of being a preposition related to the following noun, it could be an adverbial particle related to the preceding verb! Here's a sample:

"Let's clean up this situation right now!"

Your own logic tells you that the word *up* has no relationship to *situation*. You are not talking about "up the situation." Instead, *up* is related to the verb *clean*. Thus, if you were to write,

"Let's clean this situation up,"

you would not be ending your sentence with a preposition! Here's another one:

"The executives walked out into the hallway."

In this sentence, *into the hallway* is a prepositional phrase, with *hallway* the obvious object of *into*. But *out* belongs to the verb *walked* and is NOT a preposition! So if you said, *"The executives walked out,"* you would not be ending your sentence with a preposition. Got it?

Conjunctions

A conjunction is a word used to connect words, phrases or clauses within a sentence. You'll need to understand conjunctions when it comes time to punctuate your sentences, so take a moment to familiarize yourself with them.

One kind of conjunction that will affect how you punctuate your sentences is the coordinating conjunctions. These join two or more elements (words, phrases, adjectives, adverbs, pronouns, verbs, clauses, nouns) of equal rank. These are *for, and, nor, but, or, yet* and *so*.

Quick Tip! You'll need to remember coordinating conjunctions so remember this simple acronym: FANBOYS. Each letter stands for one of the coordinating conjunctions — **f**or, **a**nd, **n**or, **b**ut, **o**r, **y**et and **s**o.

Linking Adverbs With Clauses

You'll need to know these particular adverbs because they will affect how your sentences are punctuated. These adverbs are used to link clauses, and when they are at the beginning of a clause, their punctuation often causes problems for writers.

They are *consequently*, *therefore*, *thus*, *as a result*, *accordingly*, *however*, *nonetheless*, *nevertheless*, *furthermore*, *further*, *for example*, *for instance* and *namely*.

Quick Tip! You can remember the most common linking adverbs by applying the acronym LATCH, remembering that these adverbs link, or latch, clauses together. Each letter stands for a common linking adverb: *likewise*, *accordingly*, *therefore*, *consequently* and *however*.

This flyer came across your desk this morning. You'd like to attend the seminar, but the errors in the flyer make you wonder how accurate the information would be from this company. Can you find and correct the errors?

Here's a seminar that is different than all the rest. "GRAMMAR MADE REAL" is the best choice from between all the seminars out there. You'll learn how to handle grammar at every level — and inside of six hours, you'll be a grammar pro! Beside learning about nouns and verbs, you'll discover the joy of gerunds and participles, too. At this point in time, it's the best investment you can make. Where is it at? The Airport Overnight Inn is the place. Agree with attending today. Because it's the best seminar in town.

Corrections:
Here's a seminar that is different **from** all the rest. "GRAMMAR MADE REAL" is the best choice from **among** all the seminars out there. You'll learn how to handle grammar at every level — and **within** six hours, you'll be a grammar pro! **Besides** learning about nouns and verbs, you'll discover the joy of gerunds and participles, too. **Right now**, it's the best investment you can make. **Where is it**? The Airport Overnight Inn is the place. Agree **to attend** today **because** it's the

Reflections

12 REWRITING — GRAMMAR AND SENTENCES

"In all pointed sentences, some degree of accuracy must be sacrificed to conciseness."

— Dr. Samuel Johnson

"And now there abideth these three — conciseness, precision, and clarity, but the greatest of these is CLARITY!"

— (paraphrase by A.M. Moore)

The Sentence — Definition

The traditional definition of a sentence is "a group of words expressing a complete thought." Between the capital that begins your sentence and the period that ends it should be one complete thought.

If you have more than one thought or idea in a sentence, you've written a sentence that is very confusing to the reader.

"Our office records show that you are in arrears in payment although we have called you several times in order to arrange for a payment schedule that would better suit your needs, and you were supposed to consult with our housekeeping department about your needs over a week ago and failed to appear."

This sentence has two main ideas.

1. You are in arrears in your payments.

2. You were supposed to meet with the housekeeping department last week.

Not only should these two ideas occupy separate sentences, but they also should probably occupy separate paragraphs!

If you have less than a complete thought in the sentence, you have an incomplete sentence or a fragment. This is one of the most common errors that business writers make.

"All the needy children in our town."

This is incomplete since we don't know what the writer wants to say about all the needy children in our town and since it has a subject but no verb.

Writing a Complete Sentence

There is an easy way for you to determine that you've written a complete sentence. A complete sentence must have both a subject and a verb and be a complete thought.

1. **Subject**

   The subject is the *who* or *what* of the sentence. It tells you either who or what is doing the action of the verb or who or what the sentence is talking about.

   "George called home."

   The subject of this sentence is *George* since he's the one who is doing the action of calling home.

   "The needy children require assistance."

   The subject of this sentence is *the needy children* since they are the ones who need assistance.

2. **Verb**

   The verb names the action of the sentence. Remember that a verb can be a specific action, a condition or a state of being.

   "George called home."

   The verb *called* names the action being performed.

   "The needy children require assistance."

   The verb is *require* since it states the condition of the children.

3. **Complete thought**

   Remember the discussion on dependent clauses. These are groups of words that have both a subject and a verb, so they might fool you into thinking they are complete sentences. In fact, they don't complete the thought. Watch out for these since they are the most likely cause of your writing an incomplete sentence.

   "After we found the missing information."

   There is a subject *we* and a verb *found*, but the conjunction *after* indicates that more information is required to complete the thought: What happened after we found the missing information? This is a dependent clause and cannot stand alone.

Subject-Verb Agreement in Sentences

Verbs must agree with their subjects in person and number.

1. **Person**

   - The first-person subject is the person or persons speaking in a sentence *(I, we)*.

   - The second-person subject is the person or persons addressed *(you, you)*.

- The third-person subject is the person or thing spoken about and can be any noun or third-person pronoun *(he/she/it)*.

   I am   You are   It is

2. **Number**

   Verbs must agree with their subject in number, too. A singular subject takes a singular verb, and a plural subject takes a plural verb.

Singular	**Plural**
The boy runs quickly.	The boys run quickly.
She is happy.	They are happy.
I am ready to leave.	We are ready to leave.

Compound Subjects

1. **Joined by *and***

   Compound subjects joined by the conjunction *and* generally take a verb that agrees with the plural subject, even if one of the compounds is singular.

   "Three city workers and one company employee were injured in the accident."

Quick Tip! An easy way to check your accuracy with subject/verb agreement is to substitute a pronoun for the noun. *"The trains is/are late today."* Substitute the pronoun *they* for *trains* and your sentence becomes *"They are late today." Are* is the correct verb to use. *"The train and the buses is/are late today."* Substitute *they* for the compound subject: *"They are late today."*

2. **Joined by *or/nor***

Things become a little more complicated with compound subjects joined by the conjunction *or* or *nor*. The verb is plural if the subject nearest the verb is plural or if both subjects are plural.

"Were the timesheets or the memo pads ordered yet?"

Note: Both subjects are plural.

"Neither the director nor the managers were invited to the gala."

Note: The subject closest to the verb is plural.

However, if both parts of the subject are singular or if the subject next to the verb is singular, then the verb is also singular.

"The top files or the bottom drawer is the place to store the records."

Note: The subject closest to the verb is singular.

3. **With *each/every***

Compound subjects joined by *and* take a singular form of a verb when both parts of the subject have *each* or *every* preceding them.

"Each supervisor and every worker fills out the hourly sheet."

Incidentally, note that the verb in this sentence is *fills out* and that the word *out* goes with the verb, is not a preposition, and does not relate at all to *the hourly sheet*.

Other Agreement Pitfalls

1. Collective nouns

Collective nouns, like *management, staff*, etc., can take either singular or plural verbs, depending upon whether you want to emphasize the group as a whole or the individual members of the group. To make an easier choice and to ensure that your writing is correct, simply use singular verbs with collective nouns.

"The management is concerned about the policy."

"The staff is in a meeting today."

2. Phrases

If you use a phrase to add information about the subject, it can lead to confusion about the verb agreement. Block out the phrase and deal with the subject alone in order to get the right verb.

"Each of the managers is due for a raise."

The phrase is *of the managers*. When you block that out, the sentence becomes *"Each is due for a raise."* (Remember the tip for using *each*. Add the word *one* to remind you that it is singular: *"Each one of the managers is due for a raise."*

A colleague has asked you to check her work. Can you find and correct the two errors in it?

This report is in response to the questions raised by the Director of Sales. Neither the product line nor the products is at fault. The fault lies with the use of overly optimistic delivery dates by the sales staff. Either more realistic deadlines or more people on the line is needed to rectify the problem.

Corrections:
This report is in response to the questions raised by the Director of Sales. Neither the product line nor the products **are** at fault. The fault lies with the use of overly optimistic delivery dates by the sales staff. Either more realistic deadlines or more people on the line **are** needed to rectify the problem.

Reflections

13 REWRITING — MECHANICS: CAPITALIZATION, ABBREVIATION AND NUMBERS

"Writing is easy. All you do is sit staring at a blank sheet of paper until drops of blood form on your forehead."

— Gene Fowler

Style guidelines for capitalization, abbreviations and numbers are important for your business documents. As you study the guidelines here, keep in mind that your company may have guidelines for style that may vary from those given here. In general, however, most organizations accept the style in this section.

Capitalization — the 15 Basic Rules

1. **Capitalize the first word in a sentence.**

2. **Capitalize the first word of a sentence that is a direct quotation.**

   John said, "Bring me the book immediately."

3. **Capitalize each item in an outline.**

   Be sure to bring:

   - *Your book*

   - *Your pen and pencil*

   - *Your notes*

4. **Capitalize the personal pronoun "I" regardless of where it falls in a sentence.**

5. **Capitalize a complete sentence after a colon.** (If it's not a complete sentence, it doesn't require a capital.)

    "The idea is this: We bring six more packages to the meeting."

6. **Capitalize names of cities, states, provinces and countries.**

7. **Always capitalize names of races, people and languages.**

8. **Capitalize days of the week, months of the year and holidays.** Do not capitalize seasons.

    "I like to visit Vermont in the fall."

9. **Capitalize only the first word of the complimentary close of a letter.**

    "Yours truly,"

10. **Capitalize the first and last word and all important words in the titles of books, plays and newspapers.**

    "The Washington Post"

    "The Rise and Fall of the Roman Empire"

11. **Capitalize words pertaining to the Deity.**

    "God, Christ, Bible, His miracles, Buddha, Allah, Koran"

12. **Capitalize the points of the compass only when used as names of geographical regions.** Otherwise, do not capitalize.

    "He lived in the Midwest."

    "He lived in western Montana."

13. **Capitalize such words as father, mother, brother, sister, uncle and aunt only when they are used with or as proper names.**

    "I went shopping with Mother." "My mother took me shopping."

    "I went shopping with my aunt." "I went shopping with my Aunt Mary."

14. **Capitalize titles only when referring to a specific person or thing.**

    "Professor Jones taught Philosophy 101."

    "I didn't care for my professor who taught philosophy."

15. **Capitalize nicknames when they are substituted for the proper name.**

    "Chicago is known as the Windy City."

    "The Refrigerator scored ten goals in last night's game."

Abbreviations

1. **Always abbreviate:**

   - *A.D.* and *B.C.* in year dates (or *C.E.* and *B.C.E.*).

   - *a.m.* and *p.m.* in statements of time.

   - Number as *No.* before figures.

2. **Never abbreviate:**

   - *Fort*, *Mount*, *Point* and *Port* in names of places

   - Compass points in general business communications. They may be abbreviated in technical papers.

- Units of measure in general business communications (except in technical work or invoices)

  "We bought 50 pounds of the compound for our cleaning team."

3. **Avoid abbreviating:**

   - Names of streets

   - Geographical names

   - Days and months

   - Titles unless used with first and last name and the word *the*

     Reverend Smith or *the Rev. Henry Smith*

Numbers

1. **In general, spell out numbers ten and under; use figures for numbers over ten.**

   "The letter was eight pages long."

2. **If a number under ten and a number over ten appear in the same sentence, put them both in figures.**

   "There were 7 boys and 46 girls in attendance."

3. **Spell or write out large round numbers or write them in a combination of words and figures.**

   "The tanker held 23 million gallons of oil."

4. **Spell out a number if it is the first word in a sentence.**

   "Twenty-three people came to the meeting."

5. **If two numbers are part of the same construction, spell out the smaller number.**

   "Please get me 250 fifty-cent stamps."

6. **If you use numbers in a sentence in different ways, spell out numbers ten and under and use figures for the larger numbers.**

   "Within six years, he had earned over $100,000."

7. **Use words for centuries and decades when you omit the century.** Do not capitalize the words. Use figures when you give both decade and century.

   the nineteenth century   the thirties   the 1990s

8. **Write even amounts of money without decimals and zeros.** If combined with an uneven amount of money in the same sentence, write both with decimals and two places.

   "We gave $10 to charity."

   "We received a donation of $10.00 and a donation of $13.21."

9. **Use figures and words for amounts under a dollar.**

   "That cost us 35 cents."

10. **Put measurements, weights and distances in figures.**

    "Each box weighs 100 pounds."

11. **In general, express percentages in figures plus the word percent.** Use the symbol (%) in statistical or tabular material.

    "We heard from 12 percent of the respondents."

12. **Express exact age in figures.** Express approximate ages in either words or figures.

    "He is 32 today."

    "He is nearly 80."

    "She looks about fifty."

13. **Express temperature in figures with the degree sign and/or with the scale used.**

"It's nearly 40 F today."

"It's nearly 40° F today."

14. **Express time in figures with a.m. or p.m. or in words with o'clock.**

"The party begins at 5 p.m."

"The party begins at five o'clock."

Your friend gave you a travel folder that looked inviting, but after reading the fine print, you're not sure that you can trust this company to do all it promises. Can you find and correct the 12 errors in the copy?

Travel to Beautiful Tobago, an island paradise just West of

Trinidad. Plan to visit in the Winter when it's cold and snowy in

your part of the world. Be sure to put Ft. Royal on the itinerary —

it's a Fantastic Experience for Anyone. The cost is lower than

You'd expect. You'll pay only $250 per day plus $10.35 taxes for

Deluxe accommodations. 42 satisfied customers will tell you this is

a great deal for You.

Corrections:
Travel to **beautiful** Tobago, an island paradise just **west** of Trinidad. Plan to visit in the **winter** when it's cold and snowy in your part of the world. Be sure to put **Fort** Royal on the itinerary — it's a **fantastic experience** for **anyone**. The cost is lower than **you'd** expect. You'll pay only **$250.00** per day plus $10.35 taxes for **deluxe** accommodations. **Forty-two** satisfied customers will tell you this is a great deal for **you**.

Reflections

14 REWRITING — MECHANICS: PUNCTUATION

"This morning I took out a comma and this afternoon I put it back again."

— Oscar Wilde

There are two reasons to use punctuation in your business communications:

1. To present your ideas clearly and accurately

2. To indicate where one thought ends and another begins and to show how ideas relate to each other

This chapter will lay out the main uses of each kind of punctuation: period, question mark, exclamation point, comma, semicolon, colon, dash, hyphen, ellipsis, apostrophe, parentheses, brackets and quotation marks.

At the end of the chapter is a special section of Quick Tips that condenses the major points of punctuation into eight easy-to-use rules. If you're unsure of any piece of punctuation, rewrite the sentence so that it falls into the guidelines of these rules, and you'll never have to worry about a misplaced comma or incorrect semicolon again.

The Period (.)

1. **Use a period after a complete sentence when it's not an exclamation or a question.**

   "I went there. He brought the papers into the meeting."

2. **After a colon followed by a tabulated list, use a period after each member if the list contains complete sentences or independent clauses.**

   Here's what I want you to do:

   a) *Call the office in the morning.*

   b) *Arrange for a taxi to be there at nine o'clock.*

   c) *Check on the airplane reservations.*

3. **Do not use a period if the tabulated list has single words or short phrases.**

   Here's what I want you to do:

   a) *Call in morning*

   b) *Taxi*

   c) *Airplane reservations*

The Question Mark (?)

1. **Use a question mark after a direct question.**

   "What will you wear to the party?"

2. **Do not use a question mark after a polite request.**

   "Would you please pass the salt."

The Exclamation Point (!)

Beware of overusing exclamation points. Use them frugally in your writing so that when a reader sees an exclamation point, it will have the desired impact. Never put more than one exclamation point at the end of a sentence.

1. **Use with interjections.**

   "Wow!"

2. **Use after complete sentences to express extreme pleasure, excitement, enthusiasm or surprise.**

   "You really did it! That's great news!"

The Comma (,)

The comma is used so often by so many business writers that it is often used mistakenly. In fact, many writers put in a comma wherever they are unsure of the punctuation, hoping that the situation will fit one of the 26 uses of the comma!

Although there are 26 rules for the use of a comma, if you are comfortable with the ten main uses, you'll be proficient in any business writing that you undertake. Bear in mind that when the rule of comma varies between styles, you must be consistent in your use; otherwise, your reader will be unable to trust you.

1. **To separate items in a series**

   A series is at least three items in sequence. The items may be words, phrases or clauses.

   "English, geometry and physics are the key courses in that program."

The Gray Zone: Did you notice there wasn't a comma before *and* in the sentence? That's the modern way and the better way, although the rules still state that a comma before the conjunction is optional. Modern business writers only use a comma before the conjunction because it is needed to clarify the items in the series. *"The tanks were filled with sodium chloride, sodium nitrate, potassium, and sugar solution."* Without the comma after potassium, the last tank might be filled with a solution of potassium and sugar. In today's world of technical jargon, the series comma becomes the reader's best friend. Styles vary, however. For example, AP Style omits the comma because it saves newspaper space. Whatever mode you choose, BE CONSISTENT!

2. **To set off an introductory word, phrase or clause**

If the introductory phrase is short (one or two words), you don't need a comma.

"Before you can take to the slopes, you'll need to buy some new equipment."

"Yesterday morning I called the dentist."

3. **To prevent misreading**

You'll need a comma if the meaning of the sentence is different without it.

"Before testing, the boiler was dismantled."

Note: If written as *"Before testing the boiler was dismantled,"* the reader reads *"Before testing the boiler"* as an introductory phrase before realizing the phrase was supposed to be only *"Before testing."*

In any case, this sentence has a "dangling modifier," as described earlier. As it now reads, the boiler did the testing, which is ridiculous. Try it this way:

"Before it was tested, the boiler was dismantled."

Or *"The boiler was dismantled before it was tested."*

4. **To set off appositives**

If you remember, appositives give additional information about a word.

"Rudy, my secretary, will bring the papers to the office."

5. To separate a string of adjectives

Make sure that the adjectives are not cumulative — that is, their sequence can't be rearranged and still make sense.

"The report is a clear, well-designed document."

You could just as easily write, *"The report is a well-designed, clear document,"* or you could omit either adjective.

A cumulative series of adjectives should not be separated by commas. Try this one on for size!

"I am not aware of any proposed small power-producing hydroelectric generators to be connected to our system."

There you have a string of four adjectives. *Hydroelectric* modifies *generators*; *power-producing* modifies *hydroelectric generators*; *small* modifies *power-producing hydroelectric generators*, and so on. That's why they are called "cumulative."

6. To set off quotations

If a quotation appears in a sentence, set if off with commas.

Marie said, "I'd like to take a coffee break."

Then she said, "I'd also like a doughnut," and she left the room.

Don't use the single quotation marks except for a quote within a quote.

Marie said, "I never thought I would hear my boss say, 'You're fired!' to poor old Steve."

7. **To set off a clause that adds information (like appositive phrases)**

The following sentence tells us that two budgets, already checked, were approved.

"The two budgets, which had been checked, were approved."

You'll see that the reader gets a different meaning if you leave the commas out.

"The two budgets which had been checked were approved"

This sentence says that out of many budgets, only the two checked budgets were approved. What a difference two little commas can make!

8. **To set off the day of the month from the year ...**

September 26, 2000

The Gray Zone: Most grammarians say you need a comma after the year in the middle of a sentence. *"Meet me on September 26, 2000, in the lobby."* Other grammarians say it isn't needed. Follow the style of your organization. If you're in doubt, do your reader a favor and set off the year with commas as shown in the sample above.

... and to set off the state from the city

"I went to Duluth, Minnesota, to do a survey."

There's no gray zone here. As you can see, when used with the name of the city, the state is an appositive that needs to be set off from the sentence.

9. **To set off two independent clauses**

   Remember that independent clauses are, in effect, complete sentences, able to stand alone, having a subject and a verb. When they are joined together by a coordinating conjunction (remember the FANBOYS — *for*, *and*, *nor*, *but*, *or*, *yet* and *so*), the comma plus the conjunction form a necessary team.

   "I was going to the meeting, but I changed my mind."

   Notice that you use the comma only if the clauses are independent. If they're not like two complete sentences, no comma is needed.

   "I was going to the meeting but changed my mind."

   This is not a compound sentence, but instead it is a sentence that has a single subject and a compound verb.

10. **To provide a pause or to take a deep breath**

    Don't do it! Do not try to orchestrate your reader's reading by inserting commas. Altogether, there are only 26 rules for the use of commas. If you try to get "creative" with commas, your reader will go bonkers. For punctuation — go by the book.

The Semicolon (;)

Three pieces of punctuation are used to "hold" the reader at some point within the sentence. They are the semicolon, the colon and the dash. Here are the correct ways to use the semicolon.

1. **Connection without conjunction**

   A semicolon separates two closely related independent clauses that aren't joined by a conjunction.

   "I'm not good at telling jokes; I always forget the punch line."

Note: If you've ever heard of a comma splice and wondered what it was, here is the answer: If you use a comma instead of a semicolon (or a period) to join two independent clauses (or complete sentences), you've committed the cardinal grammatical error of a comma splice!

Quick Tip! If you're in doubt about this use of a semicolon, you can always make the two sentences separate by giving each one its own capital and period. The relationship between the clauses may not be as clear, but the grammar certainly will be! *"I'm not good at telling jokes. I always forget the punch line."*

2. Comma competition

A semicolon is used in place of a comma between two independent clauses joined by a coordinating conjunction (FANBOYS) if the clauses already have commas used in them.

"While coming down the aisle, Carol lost her contact lens, dropped her purse, and tripped over the step; but she managed to keep going, survive her ordeal, and make it to the altar."

Note: If the two clauses didn't already have commas in them, you'd revert to the comma rule that says you use a comma before a coordinating conjunction that joins two main clauses.

3. The sliding adverbials

When the clauses are joined by a conjunctive adverb (remember LATCH — *likewise, accordingly, therefore, consequently* and *however*), a semicolon and not a comma is used between the two clauses.

"Socrates lived long ago; however, his teachings are applied today."

You see, the "conjunctive adverb" is not a true conjunction. You can see that when you try this little experiment:

a) *"Socrates lived long ago; his teachings, however, are applied today."*

b) *"Socrates lived long ago; his teachings are, however, applied today."*

c) *"Socrates lived long ago; his teachings are applied, however, today."*

d) *"Socrates lived long ago; his teachings are applied today, however."*

Now, since in the context of this sentence, the word *but* can be substituted for the word *however*, try doing the same exercise with the word *but*. Once you slide the so-called "conjunctive" adverb away from its position following the semicolon, you find that you have the type of sentence described under #1 above.

4. **Series**

Use a semicolon if you're writing a series of equal elements, one or more of which contain internal commas.

"I plan to visit London, England; Paris, France; and Rome, Italy, on my trip."

The Colon (:)

The colon stops the reader for an express purpose: to signal that something important is coming.

1. **The colon is used after the salutation in a formal letter.**

   "Dear Sir:"

2. **The colon is used between the hour and the minute in a statement of time.**

   "8:01 p.m."

3. **The colon is used to introduce a list and must be preceded by a complete statement.** Be careful: A colon must not be used after an incomplete thought within a main sentence.

   "Many students participate in important after-school activities: the music society, the drama group and the debating club."

4. **Do not put a colon after a verb or a preposition** as this writer did.

   "Three important school activities are: the music society, the drama group and the debating club."

   "Our daughters are going to: the music society, the drama club and the swimming meet."

   In both cases, there should be no punctuation at all between the verb and its objects or between the preposition and its objects.

5. **A colon is used before listed items in outline form.** Words such as the following: *as follows*, *this*, *these* and *thus*, are most often used to introduce a list.

   The proper procedure is this:

   a) Read the entire lesson first.

   b) Study each item intensively.

   c) Study the lesson as a whole.

6. **The colon is used after a formal statement to mean, "note what follows."**

   "The citizen has one major responsibility: to vote."

7. **The colon is used between independent clauses in cases where the second clause explains the first.**

   "Our objective was clear: We had to win."

Quick Tip! If you're in doubt about this use of a colon, you can always make the two sentences separate by giving each one its own capital and period. The relationship may not be as clear, but the meaning and the grammar certainly will be! *"Our objective was clear. We had to win."*

The Dash (—) and the Hyphen (-)

These are not interchangeable, but many computer keyboards do not contain both punctuation marks. You can type two hyphens together to create a dash, but many companies will accept a *space hyphen space* combination to indicate a dash. A dash does not require any additional punctuation. If the dash is used for an emphatic setoff, a second dash is needed at the end of the setoff.

"His last name - if I ever knew it - escapes me." (space hyphen space)

"His last name--if I ever knew it--escapes me." (two hyphens)

If the setoff comes at the end of the sentence, the second dash is replaced by a period.

"His last name escapes me — if I ever knew it!"

The dash is used to express an abrupt break in thought.

"I thought I had it with me — oh no! I left it at home!"

Quick Tip! Use a dash when you mean *namely*, *that is*, *in other words* and *so on* in your explanation.

Some business writers use a dash whenever in doubt. The overuse and incorrect use of the dash lessens its value in writing.

Some consider the dash to be an informal item, inappropriate for formal writing, but most writers find it too handy to give up.

The Ellipsis (...)

1. **Use ellipsis points to indicate that material has been omitted from a quotation or quoted material.**

    "He rambled on about the importance of strong writing skills to ... one's success."

    In the above quotation, the ellipsis shows that several words from the original source have been omitted at the point where the ellipsis occurs.

2. **Use ellipsis points to show that words have been omitted at the end of a sentence.** In this case, use the ending period plus three dots.

    "He said he wasn't involved in the project ... ."

The Apostrophe (')

1. **Apostrophes are used in contractions to indicate the omission of letters.** Be aware that contractions are not considered appropriate in formal writing.

    "Let's (let us) face it. We're (we are) not going anywhere with the proposal."

Parentheses and Brackets ( ) [ ]

Parentheses are rounded and brackets are square. It is a common error to call both styles brackets. They each have a specific use.

1. **Use parentheses for incidental information.** Note that there is no punctuation before parentheses, but regular punctuation follows the parentheses.

"Call me tomorrow (Thursday), and I will give you the figures."

Note: The comma separates the two independent clauses joined by a coordinating conjunction (FANBOYS).

If the material in the parentheses requires punctuation, it is used.

"All reports must be finished this week (can you beat it!), and I haven't even started mine yet."

2. **When words in parentheses stand alone as a separate sentence, punctuate as usual with capitals and periods within the parentheses.**

   "Please return the entry blank today. (You might win a big prize!)"

3. **The only time you'll use square brackets is when enclosing descriptive information within a quote or when you insert a parenthetical remark within a larger parenthetical section.**

   "I can't believe that he [John] said that," Mary said.

   "Return your entry now! (You might win [Believe me, you might!] a wonderful prize!)"

Quotation Marks (" ")

Quotation marks seem to be a particular bane of business writers. In fact, some writers will avoid using quotations at all costs! However, there are only four rules you'll need to remember, so it's really not as bad as many people think.

1. **Use quotation marks to enclose a direct quotation: someone's exact words.**

   The shop supervisor said, "We have to deliver the product today."

2. **Always place commas and periods inside the closing quotation mark.** Place semicolons and colons outside the quotation marks.

   "The group has failed," she said.

   She said, "The group has failed."

   Look in the manual under "double-sided copying"; then follow the instructions.

   The boss considered the following as "unnecessary frills": glass mugs and gold-stamped pens.

3. **Place question marks and exclamation points inside the quotation marks if they are part of the quoted material.** If they're not part of the quoted material, but rather part of your own sentence, place them outside. Remember, use only one end mark or comma at the end of a quotation.

   Did the article say "all employees share in the plan"?

   "Why hasn't this letter been delivered?" she asked.

   Don't tell me to "keep calm"!

   "We set a new record!" Martin shouted.

4. **If you're quoting a passage that contains more than one sentence, place one quotation mark at the beginning of the quoted passage and the other one at the end of the passage.** Don't put them on each sentence in the passage.

Quick Tip Page for Punctuation!

If you're not sure of your punctuation, rewrite your sentence so that it follows one of the eight rules below. You'll notice that the rules contain the acronyms FANBOYS and LATCH. If you've forgotten them, review them in the chapter on phrases and clauses. In these rules, *sentence* means a complete sentence. It can also be an independent clause that also has a subject and verb and can be a complete sentence on its own. *Item* refers to a word, dependent clause or phrase. The *asterisk* indicates that punctuation is needed at this point. If the word *sentence* is broken up, it indicates that the sentence is interrupted for extra information, usually in the form of a dependent clause or phrase.

1. **Item * item * FANBOYS item (within a sentence)**

    Commas

    Apples, oranges and bananas are in the fruit basket.

    Send a copy to the Marketing, Finance, and Administration departments.

    You will notice that the comma before FANBOYS in the second example indicates three separate departments. Bear in mind the necessity for consistency in your writing. Since the writer of that sentence found the series comma to be necessary for clarity in that instance, she must use the series comma throughout the rest of her writing to avoid confusing her reader.

2. **Introduction * sentence**

    Commas

    Before I could call her, she called me. (A long introductory phrase needs a comma.)

    Yesterday I called her. (A short introductory phrase doesn't need a comma.)

Quick Tip Page for Punctuation! (Continued)

3. **Sentence * extra information**

   Or

   Sen * extra information * tence

   Commas

   This is Roberta, my secretary.

   Roberta, my secretary, finished the report.

4. **Sen * interruption * tence.**

   Commas or dashes or parentheses depending on the meaning

   The dog, because he wasn't tied up, bit the boy. (Extra information — same as #3)

   The dog — foaming at the mouth — bit the boy. (An abrupt break in thought)

   The dog (smaller than mine) bit the boy. (Incidental information)

5. **Sentence * FANBOYS Sentence**

   Comma

   The paper isn't ready yet, but I will have it by this evening.

6. **Se * nt * ence * FANBOYS se * nt * ence.**

   Commas and semicolon

   The dog, because he wasn't tied up, bit the boy; and the child's mother, hoping to get some money, filed a lawsuit.

Quick Tip Page for Punctuation! (Continued)

7. **Sentence * sentence**

   Semicolon

   He was a great goaltender; he never missed a shot.
   (Closely related sentences)

8. **Sentence * LATCH * sentence**

   Semicolon and comma

   *She was an expert witness; however, she didn't know
   the answers.*

Can you find the missing comma in this passage?

But the main reason for studying grammar is not "practical" at all, any more than a knowledge of astronomy or psychology or history or mathematics is mainly practical. All of these subjects have their practical applications (as does grammar) but they are not in the curriculum for the same reason that, say, driver education might be. Some academic disciplines are valuable in and of themselves.

(From: *Structures and Language of Style*, W. Ross Winterowd)

Correction:
A comma is missing after the parentheses before one of the FANBOYS.

Reflections

15 REWRITING — MECHANICS: WHICH IS THE RIGHT WORD? (COMMONLY CONFUSED WORD PAIRS)

"A general was in the habit of extending his 'most fulsome congratulations' to medal recipients. It is true that the original meaning of fulsome was 'full and abundant,' but the well-meaning general overlooked the dominant sense of the word today, 'offensive to the senses' ... ."

— Richard Lederer

Here are words you'll need to watch in your writing. Be sure to get the right one.

- **A** — an article used before a singular noun that begins with a consonant sound.

  a ball

- **An** — an article used before a singular noun that begins with a vowel sound.

  an apple   an hour

- **Aren't I** — *"I'm smart, aren't I?"* Incorrect. Plural verb used with a singular pronoun.

  Should be, *"I'm smart, am I not?"*

- **Alright, all right** — *Alright* is not a word. You wouldn't write *alwrong*, would you?

  Some writers think the expression is analogous to *already* and *all ready*, which are two separate words used for different purposes.

- **And etc.** — *Et cetera* means "and so forth." Placing *and* before it translates to *and and so forth*.

  Use *etc.* on its own. The same is true with *et al.*, short for *et alia*, which means "and others."

- **Assure, ensure, insure** — To *assure* is to speak confidently about something; to *ensure* is to make sure or to make certain; to *insure* is to protect something against loss or damage.

- **Accept, except** — *Accept* is to receive willingly; *except* is to leave out or reject.

    "We accept all credit cards except Diners Club."

- **Bring, take** — *Bring* is to bring to and *take* is to take away from.

    "Bring your spouse to the party."

    "Take the plates from the shelf."

Quick Tip! Remind yourself that fast-food restaurants frequently have a takeout window. You can take the food away from the restaurant to your home.

- **Can** — means "to be able to."

  "Can you carry those bags by yourself?" (Are you able to carry those bags?)

- **May** — means "to be permitted to."

  "May I carry those bags for you?" (Will you permit me to carry the bags?)

- **Compliment** — a comment of admiration.

    "He complimented her on her dress."

Quick Tip! Remember that the *i* in compliment means *I like something!*

- **Complement** — means "to complete."

    "The color of the walls complements the rug."

- **Compare to, compare with** — To *compare to* is to point out the similarities in different things; to *compare with* is to point out the similarities or differences in similar things.

    "Life can be compared to a rat race; rat races can be compared with rush-hour traffic."

- **Farther, further** — *Farther* has to do with distance.

    "How much farther do we have to go?"

Further usually refers to depth or intensity, but it also means "to advance or promote."

    "I plan to further your case at the board meeting."

- **Fewer, less** — *Fewer* refers to a physical number of items that you can count.

    "He ordered fewer magazines this year."

Less refers to matters of quantity or degree, among other things.

    "It was less important to me than to him."

- **Irregardless** — The word does not exist! It should be *regardless*.

- **Imply, infer** — They don't mean the same thing. To *imply* is "to suggest or indicate." To *infer* is "to reach a conclusion from the evidence at hand."

    "He implied that we would get a raise."

    "From his words, I inferred that my pay was going to get better."

- **Its, it's** — *Its* is the possessive form of *it*. It means something belongs to whatever place or thing it stands for. *It's* is a contraction for *it is*.

    "I saw the bird in its nest."

    "It's a beautiful day."

- **Presently, currently** — *Presently* means "in a little while" or "shortly." *Currently* means "going on now." Don't say *presently* when you mean "at present" or "currently."

- **Sight, cite, site** — *Sight* (noun) means "something seen." *Sight* (verb) means "to see, notice or observe." *Cite* (verb) means "to quote" or "to refer to." *Site* (noun) means "a place."

- **Verbal, spoken** — *Verbal* has been used incorrectly for a long time. Many writers use it when they mean *spoken*. *Verbal* means "expressed by words" (as opposed to hand signs or facial expression, say), either spoken or written. When you simply mean "out loud," you probably want *spoken* or *oral*.

Your assistant asked you to take a look at his memo. He's sure there's something wrong with it, but he can't figure out what it is. Can you find and correct the two errors?

TO: All staff

RE: The Office Picnic

The office picnic is scheduled for Saturday, July 14. I'm glad to report that the Weather Office has assured us the weather will be perfect. A few notes of information for you:

- It's alright to take children.

- Ensure that you have the directions to Lake Bromide. Mary has extra copies.

- Animals are not allowed, except on a leash.

- We expect fewer mosquitoes than last year.

- We require a verbal reply from each attendee, so we can order ice cream bars.

- Lake Bromide is farther than you think. Make sure your gas tank is full.

- Regardless of the weather, the picnic will go on as planned.

- Compared with last year's event, this one will be even better!

Corrections:
It's **all right** to **bring** children.

Reflections

Reflections

16 REWRITING — EDITING FOR STYLE: WORDS

"Every style that is not boring is a good one."

— Voltaire

Business writing is often cold, stiff and impersonal. Many business writers favor language that is pompous, archaic, trite and more formal than ordinary business situations require. Some favor the passive voice (*"It has been brought to our attention ... "*) over the active voice. They begin too many of their sentences with "it" (*"It has been decided that ... "*).

The most effective words are the ones you say every day. When you speak on the phone or in person, you know the words that work and those that don't. You've already tested them. Put these proven words in your writing. Write the way you speak, and your writing will be much more lively, powerful and engaging than if you write the way you think writing should sound.

Words

1. **Use short words.**

   Long words slow the reader down. Look at the words on the left-hand side of each of the columns listed on the next page. Compare how long it takes to say them with the speed of the words in parentheses.

affirmative (yes)	anticipate (expect)	cooperate (help)
determine (find)	facilitate (make easy)	forward (send)
inasmuch as (since)	indicate (show)	personnel (people)
prior to (before)	pertaining to (about)	currently (now)
request (ask)	submit (give)	terminate (end)

Using words such as the ones in the parentheses will ensure that your readers understand your message faster, easier and with fewer chances of misinterpreting what you've written.

2. Use orthodox spelling.

Writing *nite* for *night* and *thru* for *through* or *cuz* for *because* may be acceptable in a personal letter, but it has no place in business correspondence!

3. Use necessary words.

Eliminate any word that does not contribute to your message. The more unnecessary words you eliminate, the stronger and clearer your writing will become. Here are some words and phrases and their concise alternatives.

- At this point in time (now)

- For the purpose of (to)

- In the event that (if)

- Due to the fact that (because)

- In the final analysis (finally)

- Until such time as (until)

4. Use personal words.

Until recently, using words such as *I* and *we* was considered bad form in business writing. The common substitute was the word *one*. Today with business writers moving toward greater directness and simplicity in their style, *I* and *we* are not only acceptable, but they're encouraged in business writing.

Notice the difference in these two sentences:

"Of course, one cannot help regretting the incident."

"Believe me, I am very sorry that happened."

5. Use words that people like to hear.

There are many words that people like to hear in some contexts and others that they don't. Positive-sounding words help create a positive response. Compare the words people like to hear with those that turn people off.

- Achieve (blame)

- Appreciate (complain)

- Success (failure)

- You say (you claim)

- Can (impossible)

- Welcome (won't)

6. Use speaking words.

Many writers feel that they have to dress up ordinary words when they write. They want to sound learned and important, but they wind up sounding obscure and affected. Notice the difference in clarity between the pretentious phrases on the left and the simpler words in parentheses.

- Heretofore (before)

- To be in receipt of (have)

- Enclosed please find (here is)

- Commensurate with (equal to)

- Termination (end)

7. Avoid clichés.

Clichés are expressions that have been used so often that they've lost whatever energy they might once have had. Here are some clichés along with some words to consider using in their place.

- Tried and true (reliable)

- The bottom line (the deciding factor)

- Don't hesitate to call (please call)

- Few and far between (rare)

- In a nutshell (in short and to the point)

- At this point in time (now)

8. Avoid euphemisms.

Euphemisms are words and phrases meant to hide negative things. Some of them — *deceased* for *dead*, for example — may have their place, but most of them dull your style and serve no useful purpose in your business correspondence.

- Revenue enhancement (price increases)

- Negative impact (bad effect)

- Pre-owned (used)

- Contrary to expectations (unexpectedly)

9. Avoid jargon.

Using technical words or language peculiar to your special business when writing to someone outside that business guarantees that your correspondence will be misunderstood. Jargon (or buzzwords) is also a language called "business-ese." Here are some examples of this kind of jargon.

utilization	prioritization	interface
market penetration	impact (as a verb)	optimize
task (as a verb)	facilitated	

10. Avoid redundancy.

Redundant writers can't let a single word do its job — they do everything twice! *Unanimous* becomes *completely unanimous*. Here are some commonly used redundancies you'll want to avoid.

- brief in duration (brief)

- during the year 1990 (during 1990)

- resulting effect (effect)

- unresolved problem (problem)

- repeat the same (repeat)

- surplus left over (surplus)

- advance warning (warning)

- three-month period (three months)

Redundancy doesn't help clarify the meaning or enrich the style. Nevertheless, the repetition of key words and phrases can reinforce important points and enhance eloquence.

"The chief problem we face is increasing competition: competition from Japan, competition from Taiwan and competition from Germany."

11. Keep related words together.

Badly placed words and phrases can cause confusion in a sentence. Keep the words that have to do with a subject apart from those that don't. Otherwise, your writing will have a very different meaning from what you originally intended.

"The city's first sperm bank opened with semen samples from 18 men frozen in a stainless steel tank."

12. Avoid acronyms, initials and abbreviations.

Not everyone knows that SALT stands for Strategic Arms Limitation Treaty. If you want to use an acronym, write out the name fully the first time you use it, with the acronym placed in parentheses following. After that, you can use the acronym for any subsequent mention.

"The North American Free Trade Agreement (NAFTA) is entering the final negotiation stage."

13. Avoid sexist language.

Words that favor one gender over the other have no place in business writing. Such language usually occurs with third-person masculine (*he*, *him*, *himself*, *his*) and with built-in gender preferences (*chairman*, *foreman*, *stewardess*).

There are two ways to avoid sexist language:

- Use the "he or she" construction.

  "Each manager must file his or her report."

- Switch to a plural subject.

  "All managers must file their reports."

The Gray Zone: Although still seen as incorrect by some grammarians, more and more writers are using the forms of the plural pronoun *they* as a substitute for *he* or *she*. *"Each manager must file their report."* Follow the guidelines of your organization.

Avoid sexist job titles.

- Mailman (letter carrier)

- Salesman (sales representative)

- Policeman (police officer)

- Newsman (journalist)

- Fireman (firefighter)

- Chairman (chairperson or just "chair")

- Spokesman (spokesperson)

Also change sexist words that aren't necessarily job titles.

- Mankind (people)

- Manned (staffed)

- Average man (average person)

- All men (all people)

Be sure to give men and women equal treatment in how you address them.

- Men and ladies (men and women)

- Man and wife (husband and wife)

- John Dow and Mary (John and Mary Dow)

Can you find the real meaning behind these overblown phrases?

The Poor Writer's Almanac

Initially, God created the heaven and the earth.

Do it presently!

Seek and ye shall locate.

Come and obtain it.

God assists those who assist themselves.

In the event that initially you fail to succeed, endeavor, endeavor, endeavor again.

A rose by any other designation would smell as sweet.

Residence, sweet domicile.

And they lived happily ever subsequently.

All's well that terminates well.

Sufficient and to spare.

Deceased as a doornail.

— Rudolf Flesch

17 REWRITING — EDITING FOR STYLE: SENTENCES AND PARAGRAPHS

"When I see a paragraph shrinking under my eyes like a strip of bacon, I know I'm on the right track."

— Peter De Vries

Sentences

Sentences in business writing tend to be short: about 20 words or fewer. Language experts state that shorter sentences communicate information more effectively and are easier to understand. Readers want to digest information in small bits.

When you start to put your thoughts on paper, you may end up with long, complex sentences or with short, choppy ones.

Here are some formulas to help you write better sentences.

1. **Simplify your writing.**

   Look at any 150 words of your writing. Count the number of one-syllable words in the sample. Divide that number by 10 and subtract the result from 20. The number you get is the number of years of school your reader needs to read your writing easily.

   Let's say you find 60 one-syllable words in your 150-word writing sample.

   • Divide 60 by 10 = 6.

   • Subtract 6 from 20 = 14.

- This is the grade level needed to read your writing — grade 14: high school plus two years of college!

The tougher the intellectual challenge to the reader, the simpler your writing should be. If the subject is hard to understand (*Quantum Physics for Dummies!*), write one or two levels below your audience's highest reading capabilities.

What level do you think *The New York Times*, *Forbes Magazine* and *The Wall Street Journal* are written for? Grades 8 through 12.

Remind yourself that business readers want their information fast and uncomplicated.

2. Check your prefixes and suffixes.

Look for prefixes such as *pre-*, *anti-* and *multi-*. Look for suffixes such as *-ability*, *-tion* and *-ism*. See how many you can take out and replace with simpler words without sacrificing meaning.

A lawyer writes that *"the order was nondischargeable."* The root word is *charge*, but we have to process two prefixes, *non* and *dis* to get to it. Then we have to process *able* with the rest of the words. How much easier if the lawyer had simply written that *"the order couldn't be carried out."*

3. Watch the sentence length.

Write sentences that average 15-22 words and write none longer than 40 words. This is adapted from a guideline many newspapers use. Long sentences slow up comprehension because they contain too many elements that have to be related.

4. Get rid of anemic introductory phrases.

Examples of anemic introductory phrases:

- There is …

- There are …

- It appears …

- I would hope that …

These phrases say virtually nothing at all. Placing them at the beginning of a sentence takes the life out of the rest of the sentence.

"There is a difficulty with the customers paying promptly."

vs.

"Customers aren't paying promptly."

I would hope that is another weak introductory phrase. It says that the writer would like something to happen but doesn't really expect it to happen.

"I would hope that you'll get your reports in by Friday."

vs.

"Please get your reports in by Friday."

5. **Get rid of unnecessary prepositions.**

   Many business writers fill a sentence with prepositions, making the meaning cloudy and the sentence structure awkward. Compare these two versions of the same sentence, one with a lot of prepositions and the other with most of them removed.

   Tests of the machinery on the day before it was put into operation brought out defects in two of the four functions which had been specified by our shop workers. (8 prepositions in a total of 30 words)

   vs.

   Tests done the day before we used the machine showed defects in two of the four functions our shop workers had specified. (3 prepositions in a total of 22 words)

6. **Don't back into sentences.**

Backing into the sentence is starting to talk about the subject before you say what the subject is.

"Believing that significant savings can be made and that no additional time will be required for the same results, I am proposing the changes listed in this report."

The writer started with a long backing-in introductory phrase and kept the reader waiting until the end to find out what the subject was. Readers often don't bother to finish reading that kind of sentence. Keep introductory phrases short.

7. **Keep the structures parallel.**

Parallelism is a technique used in writing to combine several statements into one.

- Equal ideas in a sentence should be expressed in parallel form.

  "Mrs. Brown was not only efficient and capable but also a very conscientious person."

  Note: The word *person* destroys the parallelism of the three equal ideas about Mrs. Brown because efficient and capable are adjectives and *a conscientious person* is a noun phrase. Instead, write:

  "Mrs. Brown was not only efficient and capable but also very conscientious."

- Phrases and clauses in a series in a sentence should also be parallel in structure.

  "It is possible to go by boat or fly to the island."

  Note: The lack of parallel structure gives this sentence a decidedly different meaning from the following sentence.

  "It is possible to go by boat or by plane to the island."

- Verbs in a sentence should also be parallel in their tense structure.

  "Ted looked into the contract, talked to Hayes and finds no conflict with the former client."

  Note: The verb *finds* is in the present tense while the other two verbs, *looked* and *talked*, are in the past tense. The sentence should read:

  "Ted looked into the contract, talked to Hayes and found no conflict with the former client."

- Watch out for infinitives!

  "The corporation wants to increase productivity, to reduce costs, and improve everyone's morale."

  In this sentence, the first two infinitive verbs have the particle *to*; the third does not. To make this infinitive series parallel, either of two structures will work:

  "The corporation wants to increase productivity, to reduce costs, and to improve everyone's morale."

  Or, since the first *to* can govern the other two infinitives,

  "The corporation wants to increase productivity, reduce costs and improve everyone's morale."

The Paragraph

A paragraph consists of a group of sentences that establish and then support a specific topic. Paragraphs are like rest stops. They give the reader's eyes and mind a break. They tell the reader that it's time to take a break before going on to the next main topic.

Paragraphs can be any length. They can be as short as one sentence made up of one word!

Instead of thinking of paragraphs as having beginnings, middles and ends, use the acronym CUE to help you make your paragraphs powerful and effective.

- C — Coherence

- U — Unity

- E — Emphasis

Four Guidelines for Coherence

1. **Arrange the sentences in a logical pattern or order.**

   The order may be one of time, space, size, importance, general-to-specific or similarity-and-difference.

2. **Keep a consistent point of view.**

   Avoid shifting from one person to another, from one tense to another, or from singular to plural without a good reason.

3. **Repeat key words and phrases.**

   Or use synonyms (different words that have the same meaning). This keeps the reader's attention focused where you want it to be.

4. **Use transitional words or phrases.**

   Transitional words help the reader get from one idea to the next.

   - Words that indicate addition: *again, also, and, and then, besides, further, furthermore, moreover, in addition.*

   - Words that indicate order: *first, second, third, next, finally.*

   - Words that indicate summary: *in brief, in short, in conclusion.*

- Words that indicate example: *for example, for instance, in particular.*

- Words that indicate result: *as a result, consequently, therefore, then, thus, so, for this reason.*

- Words that indicate comparison: *similarly, in the same way as, more than, less than.*

- Words that indicate contrast: *however, nevertheless, on the other hand, yet, unlike, but, despite, in spite of.*

- Words that indicate time: *afterward, immediately, meanwhile, soon, now, at last, presently, shortly.*

Unity

Try to stick to one idea for each paragraph and place that idea in the opening sentence. Use this key sentence, called a topic sentence, to introduce or summarize your paragraph. This lets your reader know what the paragraph is about. Write the remaining sentences to support or elaborate on your main point. You can also use a topic sentence at the end of the paragraph to summarize the information contained in that paragraph.

Some writers like to use the last sentence of the paragraph to lead into the next paragraph. The closing sentence of each paragraph is the best place to form a link with the opening sentence of the next paragraph but ask yourself if you need one. If each paragraph develops a point in a series, you don't need to sum up what you've said before going on to the next paragraph.

Here are some ideas you can use for closing your paragraphs:

- Summarize the main point of the paragraph and introduce the reader to the point that will begin the next paragraph.

- Restate the paragraph's thesis if it is something you're trying to prove.

- Direct the reader's attention to the consequences of the situation described in the paragraph.

- Call upon the reader to act or tell the reader what action to take.

- End with a quotation that supports the views of the paragraph.

The last line of the last paragraph is almost as important as the opening one. Well-written endings give readers a sense of completeness. Their interest, which was aroused in the opening line and maintained in the opening lines of subsequent paragraphs, should be satisfied in the concluding line of the last paragraph. To prevent disappointing your readers:

- Do not introduce a new idea into the concluding line of your correspondence.

- Do not begin your last sentence with *in conclusion* or *to summarize.* Well-written endings are self-evident.

- Do not apologize for your opinions. You're entitled to them, and if they are substantially supported and carefully presented, you don't have to apologize for any inadequacies.

Emphasis

Begin and end each paragraph with important pieces of information and well-written sentences. This will make your reader want to continue from one paragraph to the next.

Here are some examples of the kinds of opening sentences that help maintain a reader's attention:

- Name the person or audience you're addressing.

- Begin with an answer to a question or to an opposing point of view that may be raised in the reader's mind by something you said in your previous paragraph.

- State the main idea of the paragraph in the opening sentence. Follow with the reasons why it should or should not be supported.

- Ask a question. When the reader answers it, he is involved with your subject.

- Make a prediction. You can point to the consequences of a present situation by telling your reader what will happen if he doesn't act now.

- Open with an appealing or amusing incident that will arouse your reader's curiosity.

A Final Word About Paragraphs

Construct your paragraphs with a good eye as well as a good mind. Enormous blocks of print implant in your readers' minds the image of a difficult subject. If your paragraph is too long, you may be trying to support a point that could properly be broken down into two points. Or you may be belaboring your point by excessive argument. On the other hand, a whole bunch of short paragraphs, one right after the other, can be distracting to your reader. The safest policy is to vary the length of your paragraphs. Generally speaking, the shorter the paragraphs and the fewer the number of ideas contained in them, the easier they are to read.

Use the formula to determine the reading grade level required for this article from *The Wall Street Journal*.

"When Boomers Go Bust"

By Ellen Graham

They came into the world in the full flush of postwar prosperity, jamming maternity wards to capacity and destined for a future richer and more secure than any generation before them.

But for the baby-boom generation, those rosy promises haven't fully been realized. In a high-tech, high-flux global economy that their Eisenhower-generation parents couldn't have foreseen, the 76 million Americans born between 1946 and 1964 face anxious times as the eldest among them wind down their careers.

Beginning Jan. 1, one of them will turn 50 years old every 7-1/2 seconds, "and that will continue unabated for the next 10 years," observes Joyce Welsh, a vice-president of the National Council on the Aging in Washington.

Many aging baby boomers have already been casualties of corporate retrenchment. They know that "over the hill" gets younger every year and that job survival depends on out-hustling the hungriest young co-worker. But even the most vital can't escape being part of a demographic bulge in a stripped-down workplace, and most economists envision underemployment for many of them: being cut loose from a corporate berth and taking a new, lesser job at lower pay or trading a full-time paycheck for the vagaries of self-employment.

For some, going it alone will bring the exhilaration of new careers and profitable businesses. But long-term security will be elusive, and coasting toward retirement out of the question. Some won't be retiring at all.

Reflections

18 FORM — MEMOS, BUSINESS LETTERS AND ELECTRONIC COMMUNICATION

"If a person wishes to write in a clear style, let him first be clear in his thoughts."

— Goethe

No one has to work long in the business world to discover that writing is the universal currency for documenting what gets done and for formally expressing ideas. Every businessperson is by definition a writer.

Remember that what you write is important. Business letters and memos are an indispensable part of business communication. They are used to sell products or services, request material and information, answer customer inquiries, maintain good public relations, and serve a variety of other business functions.

You may think that a lot of business would be better done over the phone, rather than in writing, but in fact, people remember only about 25 percent of what they hear. In addition, long-distance phone calls can be time-consuming and expensive. Putting it in writing remains one of the best ways to ensure that your reader gets your message.

Business letters and memos also serve as part of a company's permanent records and can also function as written contracts. As well, your letter or memo represents you and your company to people you may never meet personally. The way you express yourself and the appearance of your letter or memo leave an indelible impression on your reader's mind.

Every business letter and memo that leaves your office fulfills several purposes. As a result, each one deserves the utmost care and attention.

Getting Started

To write the most effective memos and letters, you need to do one important task before you begin: Determine what you want to say and to whom you are saying it.

Clarify your reason for writing by jotting down the purpose in one or two sentences. If you can't do this, talk it over with a colleague or rethink your position. You should be able to state the purpose of your communication before you begin to write.

Knowing your readers is as important as knowing your purpose in writing. You need to identify who they are and what motivates them.

Organizing With Letter Formulas

A number of formulas have been developed for organizing the different types of letters. You can use these formulas to help you develop your ideas before you begin to write.

1. **AIDA: A widely used formula for business sales correspondence**

   - Attention — getting the reader's eye.

   - Interest — arousing the reader's curiosity or interest in what you have to say.

   - Desire — making the reader want what you have to sell.

   - Action — showing or telling the reader what to do.

2. **IDCA: A variation of AIDA that stresses conviction or believability in your presentation.** The object is to convince the reader to act on your message.

- **I**nterest — catching the reader's eye.

- **D**esire — creating a need for your product or service.

- **C**onviction — convincing the reader that some action is required on his or her part.

- **A**ction — showing or telling the reader what to do.

3. **OFAC: Used to inform the reader of a service or product that you're offering.** Also used to solicit funds or convey information.

- **O**ccasion — telling why you are writing to the person or company.

- **F**acts — giving information needed for action on the reader's part.

- **A**ction — making a request, suggestion, statement, demand or appeal.

- **C**losing — offering additional help or information, mentioning how the reader benefits.

Formulas make it easy to keep your purpose in focus and to concentrate on the essential information.

A Guide for Writing Any Business Letter

All business letters have three things in common: a beginning, a middle and an end.

Here is a summary of the different types of letters using *B*, *M* and *E* to indicate what is appropriate in each part of the letter.

1. **Information or acceptance**

> B — State the topic or reason for the letter.
>
> M — Discuss, explain or give details.
>
> E — Indicate the action you are taking or want the reader to take.

2. **Sales or persuasion**

> B — Gain the reader's attention with an unexpected idea or offer.
>
> M — Use persuasive details or an emotional appeal to hook the reader.
>
> E — Urge the reader to act immediately and tell her what to do.

3. **Request**

> B — Tell the reader what you want.
>
> M — Explain why you want this.
>
> E — Thank the reader for her attention to this matter.

4. **Complaint**

> B — Tell the reader what is wrong.
>
> M — Provide all the details and proofs.
>
> E — Tell the reader what action you expect.

5. **Rejection**

> B — Start by empathizing with the reader.
>
> M — Bury your rejection in the middle of the letter.
>
> E — Focus on some positive aspect of the situation.

6. **Collection**

    B — Give the details of the overdue payment.

    M — Ask for immediate payment.

    E — Give consequences if payment is not received.

7. **Goodwill**

    B — Express praise, thanks, sympathy or extend an invitation.

    M — Give personal details.

    E — End on a warm note.

Organizing and Writing Memos

Memos provide a summary of important information and suggest action. They also route information, acknowledge receipt of goods or data and inform recipients on various matters.

Memos can move in all directions in a company — up, down and horizontally. You may send them to one person or to a hundred. Occasionally, they go outside the company to everyone from suppliers to governmental agencies.

By their nature, memos should be short. One or two pages are best. Memos also tend to be less formal than business letters, but that is not an excuse for producing a memo that is less than perfect in the grammar department. Give the same attention to a memo as you would to a letter to the president of your company.

Keep Your Memo Short and to the Point

Here's a simple format to follow when writing your memo:

1. Statement of purpose

Always explain your reasons for writing the memo. You may refer to a memo written and received previously, to a meeting attended, to a telephone conversation, etc. Never assume that the subject line alone is enough to indicate the purpose of a memo.

2. Message

- Enumerate main points.

- Use tables and graphs.

- Use headings and subheadings.

3. Statement of future action

Tell the reader what you want her to do or tell the reader what you are going to do. Be specific and, if possible, give a time frame for the action.

Electronic Communication

1. Faxes

Treat a fax as you would a letter or a memo. Many writers feel that the speed and ease of fax communication allows them to abdicate their responsibility for grammar or good writing. In fact, a fax is simply a faster form of letter or memo. The same amount of care should be taken as if the communication were going by standard mail. People who receive a fax make the same judgments about the writer as they do when they receive a letter or memo in an envelope.

2. E-mail

The accessibility of e-mail to people in all walks of life means that it is used for more than just business purposes. If you are e-mailing a close friend, using popular e-mail icons such as ;-) for a winking face or abbreviations such as IMHO (in my humble opinion) and LOL (laughing out loud) may be appropriate. However, in business e-mails, never use any of these shortcuts.

Remember that e-mail is read by others who look on your grammatical constructions and writing skills as a measure of the integrity and worth of both you and your company. Don't neglect to check your spelling and grammar, use proper sentences, punctuate correctly and choose the correct words. Just because the format is informal doesn't mean that the form can be incorrect.

Remember also that e-mail is considered the same as a letter. It can be used in legal transactions and, if necessary, as a source of litigation. Treat your e-mail with respect.

E-mail has become a large part of business correspondence. Give yourself this quick e-mail checkup.

	Always	Sometimes	Never
1. I find it easier to type with the "caps lock" key on.			
2. I use short forms and abbreviations in my e-mail.			
3. I send copies of my interoffice e-mails to a wide distribution list.			
4. I use my e-mail to distribute morale-building jokes and cartoons.			
5. I use my e-mail account for personal e-mail.			
6. I receive personal e-mail on my business e-mail account.			
7. I don't worry too much about spelling and grammar in e-mail since it's just a form of speaking.			
8. I don't think anyone really looks at grammar and spelling in e-mail.			
9. I don't worry that my e-mail might be passed on to others.			
10. I just let my e-mail pile up and hope I can find what I need when I need it.			

Note: Each of the above is a legitimate concern with e-mail etiquette and use. If you checked "always" for any statement, you'll need to reconsider how you use your e-mail in that circumstance.

Reflections

19 FORM — FORMAL REPORTS

At some point in your business career, you may be called on to write a long or formal report on an assigned topic at the request of management. This is an opportunity for you to shine.

The formats of reports vary from company to company. However, most long or formal reports have 11 elements. Not every report will contain all 11 parts. You may want to omit some part, depending on the kind of report and on your readers' needs; nonetheless, you should be aware of the purpose and function of each part.

The 11 parts can be divided into *preliminary materials*, *body of the report* and *supplemental materials*.

Preliminary Materials

1. **Title page**

   The title page contains all the identifying information.

   - Title of the report

   - Issuing company

- Recipients

- Date

- Writer's name

Most companies have their own formats for title pages so check copies of previous reports to see which format your company uses.

2. Letter of authorization

This letter follows a blank sheet of paper after the title page and is keyboarded according to the company format for business letters. The person who authorized the report should write the letter. It should outline the purpose or importance of the material and should authorize the research and writing of the report.

3. Letter of transmittal

This letter, in the form of a regular business letter or memo, addresses the receiver of the report and explains the purpose of the report. It may contain a checklist of all persons who will receive a copy of the report.

4. Table of contents

The table of contents lists all the topics and materials in the report. Use lowercase Roman numerals to number all the preliminary report materials, except the title page. Number the body of the report with Arabic numerals. Each company may have a slightly different format for the table of contents. Check previous reports to establish the format.

You may put the table of contents in uppercase and lowercase or in all capitals. You may want to list the titles of appendices by letter. You will indent the appendix titles under the heading "Appendices."

5. Synopsis or summary

Other terms you can use for this section of the report are *preface*, *abstract*, *forward* or *digest*. This section gives the reader a quick, concise overview of the report. It is usually one-half-page to one-page long and does not include data or figures.

A good summary:

- Provides enough information to specify the aims and results of your project

- Is brief without omitting essential information

- Is written in a fluid, easy style

- Is consistent in tone and emphasis with the body of the report

- Makes use of accepted abbreviations to save space but does not include any tables or illustrations

Body of the Report

6. Introduction

The introduction describes the reason for the report. It contains the purpose, methods of gathering data, sources, definitions and a brief plan of the report. A good introduction arouses the readers' interest and gives some background information on the subject, preparing them for the contents of the report.

7. Body

Include in this section all the pertinent data you have gathered and analyzed. State your case and substantiate your points, presenting the results of your research and analysis. You may also include illustrations — charts, graphs, pictures — to support or enhance your discussion.

Organize your report under various headings. Major headings indicate the main points of the report. Subheadings and sub-subheadings indicate subordinate and supporting ideas. You'll notice that this use of headings is similar to the traditional outline that you learned to make in your early grammar classes. Where you place the various categories and headings will depend on your company's preference, but in general, follow these guidelines:

- First category — centered, in capitals

- Second category — left margin, in capitals

- Third category — left margin, initial capitals, underscored

- Fourth category — indented five spaces from left margin, initial capitals, underscored

- Fifth category — left margin, initial capitals

Generally, you'll need only three categories; however, you can use additional headings if necessary.

Here is a general outline of where to put the various elements on the page:

- Page numbers — Number second and succeeding pages either at the top center or top right-hand side, four lines from the top of the page. Alternatively, you may place page numbers at the bottom center or right-hand side, approximately four lines from the bottom of the page.

- Major heading — center and capitalize

- Subheading — left margin, capitalize

- Margins — left margin, 1-1/2 inches; right margin, 1 inch; 1-inch to 1-1/2-inch top and bottom margins

- Body of report — double-space

- Long quotes, etc. — single-space long quotes, end footnotes, tables and bibliographies

Footnotes — There are two styles of footnotes: the American Psychological Association (A.P.A.) style and traditional style.

- The A.P.A. style is most commonly used since it is the easiest to keyboard. Simply put the author and year of publication after the reference in the body of your report and then place the full bibliographical reference in the bibliography.

  Entry in body of report:

  Peter Drucker was the first person to use the term "management by objectives" (Drucker, 1954).

  Entry in bibliography:

  Drucker, Peter. (1954). The practice of management. New York: Harper and Row.

- The traditional style uses a small superscript (above the middle of the line) number in the body of the report, and then you place the full bibliographical reference at the bottom of the page. Most keyboards are not set up to handle superscript numbers.

Endnotes — Use endnotes when you are writing articles for magazines and trade journals or authoring books. Throughout the chapter, use superscript numbers, just as you do with traditional footnotes; however, instead of placing the bibliographic reference or additional information at the foot of the page on which you put in the superscript number, prepare a set of endnotes on the last page of the chapter or article.

8. Conclusion

Readers may skim through the body of the report to get to the conclusion section. They want to know what the data and supportive materials mean. What patterns, trends or observations did you find in your research? You should state your conclusions briefly and clearly, preferably in a series of numbered statements. Make sure that your conclusions are logical outcomes of your data, supported by the information and research you have completed.

9. Recommendations

Take your conclusions to the next step and answer such questions as:

- What should be done?

- How do we achieve the desired outcome?

- How can we persuade people to agree with our plan of action?

Your recommendations should be action steps or suggestions for action that give the readers a starting point for the next phase in the process.

Supplementary Materials

10. Bibliography

List in the bibliography all sources used in writing your report. List the names of people you've interviewed or with whom you have corresponded. Give the complete information on all books, reports, articles, documents and other references so that your readers can locate and review these materials if they wish.

Alphabetize entries in the bibliography by the author's last name or by the document's title if there is no author. Articles *an*, *a* and *the* are not used as the first word.

11. Appendices

Include in this section information that supports the data in the body but is too lengthy or detailed to include in the text. You can include charts, questionnaires, short reports or documents, photographs, explanations of statistical methods or computer programs used to gather data, transcripts of interviews, or any other data you feel the reader would find valuable.

Illustrations

1. Graphs

- Visually more interesting than tables

- Easy for the reader to spot trends, cycles and other movements

- Condense a large amount of material into a small space

2. Tables

- Present information in columns

- Summarize changes or compare information over time

- Include more detailed or complex material than graphs

- Contain some narrative or explanation

3. Photographs

- Good when discussing site locations or new facilities

- Excellent for showing damage for insurance purposes

Note: Number illustrations consecutively within a chapter or throughout the report if you do not have chapters. Give them a designation: Table 1 or Illustration 3.

Ask to see some of your company reports. Check them for style and layout. Are they consistent with the outlines given in this chapter or are there particular style differences that you should be aware of? Make notes of the preferred report style of your company.

Reflections

20 FORM — RÉSUMÉS

Your résumé may be the most important piece of writing that you ever do. For that reason, it's vital that it be correct in every way: grammar, syntax, form, style and appearance. It will represent you to a future employer.

You can have several résumés — each one in a format that fits a particular need. One might highlight your writing skills, another might summarize your management abilities and experience, and still another may emphasize your teamwork. Research the companies that interest you, and tailor your résumé to their job requirements. The more exactly you fit the requirements of the job, the more likely you are to secure it.

Five Important Considerations

1. **Avoid any mention of membership in a specific religious or political organization.** Unless you are applying for a position that requires this membership, don't include information that may bias an employer before you have secured an interview.

2. **Don't include a photograph unless specifically asked to do so by the organization.**

3. **Don't mention money.** The discussion of salary can wait until the job interview.

4. **Attempt to stress your accomplishments in terms that will show the employer you are responsible, dependable and able to work independently and cooperatively with others.**

5. **Ensure that your résumé is accurate and concise.** Since many résumé readers base their judgments on a quick look, be sure that the résumé is easy to read and to the point. Make sure it is correct!

Formatting Résumés

There are no fixed rules for résumé format and layout, but you should plan your résumé so that it is clear, concise and readable. There are two basic types of résumés: the *chronological* and the *functional*.

1. **The chronological résumé:**

    • Lists the jobs you have held and their responsibilities, usually following a sequence of dates

    • Details work experience in reverse chronological order and includes education

    • Is easiest to prepare and is most favored by organizations — preferred by 83 percent of corporate human resource professionals

2. **The functional résumé:**

    • Focuses on your accomplishments and the skills you have acquired

    • Focuses on a position/job target

    • Presents capabilities in support of that position

    • Permits you to prominently relate your ability to do the job even if skills and experience are not recent

    • Includes job titles and dates of employment

When using this form, you must research the position you are seeking in order to fit your résumé to that specific job.

3. **Scannable résumés**

These are designed to be entered into a computerized database. The résumé is read by a scanner and stored in text format. E-mail résumés also deserve special attention to ensure an organized transfer of your information.

The Elements of a Chronological Résumé

The elements of a résumé are fairly standard, though they can be arranged to minimize and maximize elements of your work history (or lack thereof).

1. **Basics**

Include your name, address, phone number and e-mail address. Note: It is unnecessary to list your age, marital status, state of health, birthdate, height or weight.

2. **Objective**

This is a one- to two-sentence statement of your career goal. It's optional, but many employers expect to see it. Don't just repeat the job description from an ad. An alternative is an employment profile, where you wrap up you and your skills in one or two sentences. Your whole résumé should make your objective clear, with or without the opening tagline.

3. **Education**

List your highest degree awarded, dates of attendance, major or concentration, grade-point average overall or in your major (again, optional, but employers may inquire), study-abroad programs, honors received and other programs. Include special projects only if relevant and your high school only if it's a strong selling point.

4. Special skills

Make note of proficiency in foreign languages, computer knowledge or proficiency, and any other information you believe is relevant or makes you a more interesting candidate.

5. Activities

List professional affiliations, interests, volunteer work and anything else you think is relevant or shows your personality. Often an interviewer will focus on your activities to get a sense of who you are.

6. Experience

Include internships, summer jobs, relevant volunteer work and any other applicable experience. If you're using a traditional résumé, place these items in reverse chronological order. Include your job title, the company's name and location, your dates of employment and major duties.

Be sure you account for any obvious gaps in your work history; for example, you may have returned to school, stayed at home to care for small children, traveled or undergone medical treatment.

7. References

It's sufficient to say that references are available upon request, as long as you're prepared to supply them at some point. Obviously, it's in your best interest to ask only those individuals for references who will speak glowingly of you and your abilities. If you're in any doubt about what the person might say about you, be sure to ask. If you've lost a job or left it under less than desirable circumstances, it's worth your while to find out exactly what this employer would say about you if asked. If you know in advance of the job interview that you may receive an unfavorable reference, you can deal with it on your own terms at the time of the interview.

The Functional Résumé

This résumé is similar to the chronological résumé except that it downplays the experience section, summarizing it in a short paragraph or two. Instead, this résumé focuses on achievements or areas of accomplishments. It's important to know your own strengths and to make sure that the list of accomplishments reflects them.

The following is a list of some action words that you may want to incorporate into your functional résumé. If you are writing about an activity that occurred in the past, use the simple past tense (*budgeted*). If the activity is occurring now, use the simple present tense (*budget*).

achieved	acquired	adapted	addressed	administered
analyzed	anticipated	assembled	assisted	audited
budgeted	calculated	centralized	changed	collaborated
composed	condensed	conducted	constructed	contracted
converted	coordinated	created	cultivated	demonstrated
designed	developed	devised	discovered	doubled
drafted	edited	eliminated	enforced	established
evaluated	expanded	explained	forecasted	formed
founded	generated	hired	implemented	improved
informed	insured	interpreted	interviewed	launched
maintained	managed	marketed	minimized	motivated
negotiated	obtained	operated	organized	originated
oversaw	performed	planned	prevented	produced
promoted	provided	publicized	published	recruited
reorganized	reported	researched	resolved	reviewed
selected	separated	simplified	solved	supervised
surveyed	taught	tested	trained	utilized

Résumé Resources

There are a number of sites on the World Wide Web that are geared specifically to the résumé writer. Most of them contain samples of résumés and ideas for making your résumé more powerful. Search under *how+to+write+resumes+online+resources* for an up-to-date listing of some of the better sites.

Take some time to update and edit your résumé. Although you may not be seeking a new position in another company, many organizations will ask for a résumé when considering you for a promotion to another position within the same company.

Be sure to look at some of the résumé-writing resources that are available, either through books or on the World Wide Web.

Using this handbook, double-check grammar, spelling, punctuation, style and tone. Remember, this could be the most important document that you will ever produce.

Reflections

INDEX

NOTES

YOUR BACK-OF-THE-BOOK STORE

ORDER FORM

Because you already know the value of National Press Publications Desktop Handbooks and Business User's Manuals, here's a time-saving way to purchase more career-building resources from our convenient "bookstore."

- IT'S EASY … Just make your selections, then visit us on the Web, mail, call or fax your order. (See back for details.)
- INCREASE YOUR EFFECTIVENESS … Books in these two series have sold more than two million copies and are known as reliable sources of instantly helpful information.
- THEY'RE CONVENIENT TO USE … Each handbook is durable, concise and filled with quality advice that will last you all the way to the boardroom.
- YOUR SATISFACTION IS 100% GUARANTEED. Forever.

60-MINUTE TRAINING SERIES™ HANDBOOKS

TITLE	YOUR PRICE*	QTY.	TOTAL
8 Steps for Highly Effective Negotiations #424	$14.95		
Assertiveness #4422	$14.95		
Balancing Career and Family #4152	$14.95		
Diversity: Managing Our Differences #412	$14.95		
The Essentials of Business Writing #4310	$14.95		
Exceptional Customer Service #4882	$14.95		
Fear & Anger: Control Your Emotions #4302	$14.95		
Fundamentals of Planning #4301	$14.95		
Getting Things Done #4112	$14.95		
How to Coach an Effective Team #4308	$14.95		
How to De-Junk Your Life #4306	$14.95		
How to Handle Conflict and Confrontation #4952	$14.95		
How to Manage Your Boss #493	$14.95		
How to Supervise People #4102	$14.95		
How to Work With People #4032	$14.95		
Inspire and Motivate: Performance Reviews #4232	$14.95		
Listen Up: Hear What's Really Being Said #4172	$14.95		
Motivation and Goal-Setting #4962	$14.95		
A New Attitude #4432	$14.95		
The New Dynamic Comm. Skills for Women #4309	$14.95		
Parenting: Ward & June… #486	$14.95		
The Polished Professional #4262	$14.95		
The Power of Innovative Thinking #428	$14.95		
The Power of Self-Managed Teams #4222	$14.95		
Powerful Communication Skills #4132	$14.95		
Present With Confidence #4612	$14.95		
The Secret to Developing Peak Performers #4962	$14.95		
Self-Esteem: The Power to Be Your Best #4642	$14.95		
Shortcuts to Organized Files and Records #4307	$14.95		
The Stress Management Handbook #4842	$14.95		
Supreme Teams: How to Make Teams Work #4303	$14.95		
Thriving on Change #4212	$14.95		
Women and Leadership #4632	$14.95		

TITLE	RETAIL PRICE	QTY.	TOTAL
The Assertive Advantage #439	$26.95		
Being OK Just Isn't Enough #5407	$26.95		
Business Letters for Busy People #449	$26.95		
Coping With Difficult People #465	$26.95		
Dealing With Conflict and Anger #5402	$26.95		
Hand-Picked: Finding & Hiring… #5405	$26.95		
High-Impact Presentation and Training Skills #4382	$26.95		
Learn to Listen #446	$26.95		
Lifeplanning #476	$26.95		
The Manager's Role as Coach #456	$26.95		
The Memory System #452	$26.95		
Negaholics® No More #5406	$26.95		
Parenting the Other Chick's Eggs #5404	$26.95		
Taking AIM On Leadership #5401	$26.95		
Prioritize, Organize: Art of Getting It Done 2nd ed. #4532	$26.95		
The Promotable Woman #450	$26.95		
Sex, Laws & Stereotypes #432	$26.95		
Think Like a Manager #451	$26.95		
Working Woman's Comm. Survival Guide #5172	$29.95		

SPECIAL OFFER:
Orders over $75 receive
FREE SHIPPING

Subtotal	$
Add 7% Sales Tax	
(Or add appropriate state and local tax)	$
Shipping and Handling	
($3 one item; 50¢ each additional item)	$
Total	$
VOLUME DISCOUNTS AVAILABLE — CALL 1-800-258-7248	

Name_____Title_____

Organization _____

Address_____

City _____State/Province _____ZIP/Postal Code _____

Payment choices:
❏ Enclosed is my check/money order payable to National Seminars.
❏ Please charge to: ❏ MasterCard   ❏ VISA   ❏ American Express

Signature _____Exp. Date _____Card Number _____
❏ Purchase Order #_____

MAIL: Complete and mail order form
with payment to:
National Press Publications
P.O. Box 419107
Kansas City, MO 64141-6107

PHONE:
Call toll-free **1-800-258-7248**

INTERNET: http://www.natsem.com

FAX:
1-913-432-0824